LABOR AND LIBERALIZATION

A SERIES OF TWENTIETH CENTURY FUND/CENTURY FOUNDATION REPORTS examining the key issues post-Soviet Russia faces as it makes the change from communism to a market economy and struggles to find its place in the world.

RUSSIA IN TRANSITION

LABOR AND LIBERALIZATION

TRADE UNIONS IN THE NEW RUSSIA

LINDA J. COOK

A TWENTIETH CENTURY FUND REPORT

THE CENTURY FOUNDATION

1997 • The Twentieth Century Fund Press • New York

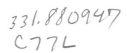

Library of Congress Cataloging-in-Publication Data

Cook, Linda J., 1952–
  Labor and liberalization: trade unions in the new Russia / by Linda J. Cook.
    p.   cm. -- (Russia in transition)
  "Twentieth Century Fund report."
  Includes bibliographical references and index.
  ISBN 0-87078-377-7
  1. Trade-unions--Russia   (Federation)   2. Labor movement--Russia (Federation) 3. Russia (Federation)--Economic conditions--1991-
I. Title.   II. Series.
HD6735. 15. C66 1997
331.88'0947--dc21   97–8847
                                                               CIP

Cover design and illustration: Claude Goodwin
Manufactured in the United States of America.
Copyright © 1997 by the Twentieth Century Fund, Inc. All rights reserved. No part of this publication may be reproduced, stored in a retrieval system, or transmitted, in any form or by any means, electronic, mechanical, photocopying, recording, or otherwise, without the prior written permission of the Twentieth Century Fund, Inc.

FOREWORD

There's a special poignancy about American assistance to the new Russia. We want to help Russians have fair and open elections, free from corruption and special interest manipulation; we offer support for vigorous market capitalism, with its promise of prosperity for virtually everyone; and we give advice and encouragement to further the evolution of broadly based, democratic, and vital labor unions that will ensure a fair share for all workers. In short, we want Russians to have the courage of our convictions.

We are, of course, making these efforts at a time when the ultimate character of the new Russian Federation is scarcely discernible. After all, three transformations are taking place simultaneously: the swift embrace of a dramatically more democratic form of government, the great leap from a command to a market economy, and the stunning withdrawal from a worldwide military standoff with the United States.

In view of this unsettled situation, the Trustees of the Twentieth Century Fund supported the notion of a special series, Russia in Transition, to examine selected topics from the extensive public policy agenda related to the changes taking place in the new Russia. Our initial report, *Ecological Disaster: Cleaning Up the Hidden Legacy of the Soviet Regime* by Murray Feshbach, was published early in 1995. Over the past two years, we have produced two more volumes in the series: Kevin O'Prey's *A Farewell to Arms? Russia's Struggles with Defense Conversion* and, most recently, Glenn E. Schweitzer's *Experiments in Cooperation: Assessing U.S.-Russian Programs in Science and Technology*.

In this, the latest in the series, Linda Cook, associate professor of political science at Brown University, draws a detailed roadmap of the current structure, politics, and prospects of organized labor in Russia. She also reports and comments on the efforts by various Western governments, unions, and international organizations to provide help in labor law reform. Some initiatives, such as projects to strengthen the "rule of law," have been important in recasting the basic framework both of unions themselves and of their relations to the state and employers. Others are scarcely relevant to a situation in which workers are routinely unpaid, often for weeks or months at a time; in such cases, strikes are essentially about the most basic aspects of working conditions.

The central fact of Russian labor is that, while there has been some significant evolution in practices, the continued dominance of the Federation of Independent Trade Unions (FNPR), successor to the old Communist worker organization, ensures that change will not come easily. The FNPR leadership has a stake in maintaining long-standing relationships with the managers of large Russian businesses, usually the same executives who directed matters in the Soviet Union (and who today are, in many cases, the most substantial shareholders in their privatized institutions). Even with falling wages and considerable worker discontent, alternative unions represent only about 10 percent of the organized workforce.

A second compelling fact of union life is that the movement of many workers from old industries to new ventures is unlikely to strengthen the hand of rank-and-file workers. In most cases, these new businesses are not unionized, so their growth reduces overall unionization. Cook argues, moreover, that prospects for future unionization in this new private sector seem very poor. These circumstances are all too familiar to students of labor in the United States.

In fact, the United States is not the most important model for unions in Russia. Nor does it provide the only direct assistance for the transformation process under way. The International Labor Organization (an arm of the United Nations) and its affiliate, the International Confederation of Free Trade Unions, are both active along with the AFL-CIO. The path to the sort of "tripartism" (government, labor, industry) that is common in Western Europe would seem far easier as a course for Russian unions than the modern, embattled American version of unionization.

Cook also looks at the small but genuine accomplishments of Westerners working with the Russian rank and file, particularly in teaching them how to organize and in helping to create labor laws. But given meager U.S. political support for foreign aid of any kind—much less for assistance to unions, of all things, and in Russia, of all places—Cook does not anticipate big payoffs from these limited efforts. She does suggest, however, that AFL-CIO assistance efforts should no longer be confined to helping the small, independent unions. This might be the moment to engage the FNPR directly. Indeed, seminars introducing the concept of democratic unionism and leadership accountability to FNPR unions could help to spur new patterns of behavior, yielding a much bigger pay-off because of their overwhelming size.

In the last analysis, Russian workers may need unions even more than do their counterparts in developed capitalist democracies. The "Wild West" character of present Russian markets makes the value of, if you will, a posse of workers obvious.

RICHARD C. LEONE, *President*
The Twentieth Century Fund
April 1997

Contents

ACKNOWLEDGMENTS

Many people contributed to the writing of this book. My first thanks go to Greg Anrig of the Twentieth Century Fund for proposing the project; to the Fund's reviewers, Brewster Denny and Steven Greenfield, for comments and suggestions that greatly improved the original draft; and to Steven Greenfield for his excellent editorial work.

This study could not have been written without the cooperation of many individuals in American, Russian, and international trade union organizations who agreed to be interviewed, and who gave generously of their time and knowledge. Here I want to thank especially Daniel Rosenblum and Ellen Hamilton of the Free Trade Union Institute, as well as the many others mentioned in the references. International aid efforts are often viewed cynically these days, but I was repeatedly impressed by the thoughtfulness of those with whom I spoke, their deep knowledge of the conditions of unions and workers in Russia, and their determination to make some sustainable impact.

Many others deserve thanks. For comments on all or part of the manuscript, I am grateful to Walter Connor, Valentin Peschanski, Patrick Collins, and Janine Ruth Wedel. Victor Komarovsky and Anna Valcheva provided invaluable research assistance. Paul Gordon gave me critical advice and enthusiastic support at various stages. The Russian Research Center (now Davis Center for Russian Studies) at Harvard University provided a congenial and collegial research environment. I am especially grateful to Vladimir Gimpelson, who taught me a great deal about Russian labor and economic reform. As always, the Center's librarians, Susan Gardos and Helen Repina, guided me to critical sources.

While writing the manuscript I also benefited from participation in the Seminar on Economic and Political Transitions held at Brown University's Watson Institute, at which an eclectic and stimulating group of colleagues discussed simultaneous economic and political transitions in theory and practice. The seminar discussed some pieces of the manuscript and many more broadly relevant themes. Of those attending I would like to mention especially Thomas Biersteker, Corina-Barbara Francis, Marsha Pripstein-Posusney, and Marilyn and Dietrich Rueschemeyer.

While I am grateful to all those named above, it goes without saying that responsibility for the final product rests entirely with myself.

My deepest thanks go to my husband, Dan, and our son, David, who was born in the midst of this project. This book is dedicated to them. David contributed to many delays in the writing (about which the Fund was most understanding), but I wouldn't wish it otherwise.

LIST OF ABBREVIATIONS

ABA	American Bar Association
AFT	American Federation of Teachers
AID	Agency for International Development
AIFLD	American Institute for Free labor Development
AFL-CIO	American Federation of Labor-Congress of Industrial Organizations
CPRF	Communist Party of the Russian Federation
CSCE	Commission on Security and Cooperation in Europe
EI	Education International
ESEUR	Education and Science Employees' Union of Russia
EU	European Union
FNPR	Federation of Independent Trade Unions of Russia (*Federatsiia Nezavisimykh Profsoiuzov Rossii)*
FPAD	Federation of Air Traffic Controllers' Unions (*Federatsiia Profsoiuzov Aviadispetcherov*)
FPALS	Federation of Unions of Civil Aviation Flight Personnel (*Federatsiia Profsoiuzov Letnogo Sostava*)
FSU	Former Soviet Union
FTUI	Free Trade Union Institute
GKI	State Committee for the Management of State Property
ICFTU	International Confederation of Free Trade Unions
ILO	International Labor Organization
IMF	International Monetary Fund
KTR	Confederation of Labor of Russia (*Konfederatsiia Truda Rossii*)
NED	National Endowment for Democracy
NPG	Independent Miners' Union (*Nezavisimyi Profsoiuz Gorniakov*)
OECD	Organization for Economic Cooperation and Development
PIER	Partners in Economic Reform

RAFTURE Russian-American Foundation for Trade Union Research
          and Education
ROPP   Russian United Industrial Party (*Rossiiskaia Obedinennaia
          Promyshlennaia Partiia*)
Sotsprof Association of Social Trade Unions
TACIS   Technical Assistance to the Commonwealth of
          Independent States
UMW   United Mine Workers of America
VKT   All-Russian Confederation of Labor (*Vserossiiskaia
          Konfederatsiia Truda*)
VTsSPS   All-Union Central Council of Trade Unions (*Vsesoiuznyi
          Tsentral'nyi Sovet Profsoiuzov*)

INTRODUCTION

In the summer of 1989, Soviet miners launched a massive strike move-ment. Built on grassroots activism, coordinated, and disciplined, the strikes seemed to indicate an enormous and unexpected capacity for organization on the part of workers. The miners repudiated the old, state-dominated official unions and set up workers' committees that later spawned a new Independent Miners' Union (NPG). The strikers sup-ported important elements of Mikhail Gorbachev's economic reform program, demanding that the mines be granted economic independence from the state in the belief that the sector would prosper once they con-trolled the marketing and sale of coal. The miners also displayed confi-dence in newly emerging democratic institutions. They timed their strike to coincide with the first meetings of the Congress of People's Deputies, the Soviet Union's first elected legislature, and looked to the Congress and the government for redress of grievances. Breaking with his prede-cessors' repressive stance toward labor activism, Gorbachev negotiated with the miners and agreed to meet most of their demands. There was a tremendous sense of workers' empowerment and optimism for the growth of a democratic labor movement in Russia.

In retrospect, the 1989 strikes look more like the high point than a beginning for the labor movement. Activism did continue among the miners; indeed, another series of strikes in 1991 helped precipitate the collapse of the Soviet Union. But the NPG continues to organize only a small percentage of miners, and strong, new independent unions have emerged in just a few additional sectors of the labor force. The Federation of Independent Trade Unions (FNPR), the successor of the old official unions, remains by far the largest, with more than 90 percent of all union-ized workers.* The miners' expectations of benefiting from reform have

---

* The terminology here is confusing because both the FNPR and the new unions label themselves "independent." I will use the term "successor" to refer to unions that remain within the FNPR and "independent" to refer to new unions as well as a few that have broken away from the FNPR and democratized.

been largely disappointed by economic realities. Prospects for the profitable marketing of Russian coal have proved limited both domestically
and abroad. Many of the mines cannot survive without state subsidies
and face closure. The government has from the beginning delivered poorly on its promises and now often fails to pay either wages, or debts (for
coal consumed by state-funded institutions and organizations), for
months at a time. Miners are reduced to negotiating for resettlement aid
for those laid off and holding brief, sporadic strikes to demand payment
of back wages. In other sectors of Russia's labor force as well activism
has brought only limited or temporary gains and has become increasingly defensive and ineffective in the face of market reforms and macroe-
conomic stabilization policies. Levels of organizing and collective action
remain low.

Workers do have other means for voicing their interests within the
Russian Federation government. Unions, both independent and successor, hold seats on the Tripartite Commission for the Regulation of Social
and Labor Relations, where they bargain with representatives of management and government ministries over economic policy. They can also
lobby the legislative committees of the Russian parliament, the Duma,
and seek to influence electoral outcomes through endorsements and
alliances. But each of these means has provided meager influence. The
Tripartite Commission has frequently been mired in conflict, including
disputes between independent and successor unions over rights to represent workers. The commission's annual General Agreements on Social
and Economic Policy tend to be vague and badly implemented, and regularly result in mutual charges of bad faith between unions and government. The unions have had somewhat more success in legislative politics,
but conflicts between legislature and executive have left many measures
in limbo. Here too, independent and successor unions frequently pursue
conflicting interests and agendas. In electoral politics unions have frag-
mented, spreading their endorsements across the political spectrum and
in any case generally exercising little influence on their members' votes.
Repeated attempts to form European-style labor or social-democratic
parties have proved abortive.

At the enterprise level Russian unions have many new formal rights,
in part a result of their own efforts to liberalize labor legislation. Indeed,
reform of legislation on labor and industrial relations has been one area
of real progress. Current labor law gives workers an unqualified right to
form new unions. All unions have the right to engage in collective bargaining with management, to go to arbitration if bargaining fails, and to
have collective wage and other agreements enforced. Most have the right

to strike. While some workers and unions have used these rights effectively, however, abuses are rampant. Activists who seek to form new unions are often dismissed or otherwise penalized by managers. Managements commonly refuse to bargain with unions, or ignore agreements they have made. The successor unions, entrenched in enterprises, try to close out independent challengers, which often must engage in lengthy litigation to survive. There are periodic reports of violence against activists.

In sum, Russia's unions are weak, and they have provided poor defense for workers in the face of economic reform and transition to the market. Average real wages have fallen to about 70 percent of their pre-reform level, while income disparities have increased markedly. A quarter of the population have incomes below the official poverty level, and more than half the national monthly wage bill is in arrears. Unemployment is increasing; whereas the official level remains a comparatively modest 9 percent, significant numbers also belong to the "hidden unemployed"—those sent on unpaid administrative leaves or employed part-time by faltering enterprises. A privatization program that was designed to give workers a sizable share in the ownership of their enterprises has instead left power mainly in the hands of managers, who often bought substantial shares at bargain-basement prices and can now restructure with little input from unions and little concern for their workers' interests. The social safety net that should provide unemployment insurance, retraining, job referral services, and an income floor for those displaced by reform is sorely inadequate. For the minority of skilled and educated workers who can move into jobs in the new, highly paid private sector, reform has brought real benefits. For the majority, though, the costs have been great. Some of these costs are of course inevitable if Russia is to make the transition to a more efficient, market-oriented economy. But in a democratizing society, if the costs become intolerable, reform may not survive.

Russian workers have in fact taken their discontent with reform to the ballot box. In the December 1993 Duma elections large numbers turned away from the government-sponsored program to support Communist, nationalist, and other antireform parties. Vladimir Zhirinovsky's extreme nationalist Liberal Democratic Party placed second, with significant support from workers.[1] Though Zhirinovsky's fortunes have since waned, the Communist Party of the Russian Federation (CPRF), promising to restore full employment as well as free education and health care, to hold down prices, and to renationalize bankrupt enterprises, placed first in the December 1995 Duma elections with more than 22 percent of the vote, making it by far the largest party in the Russian legislature. In the first round of the 1996 presidential election CPRF leader Gennady Zyuganov got 24 million votes, 32 percent of the electorate, against Boris Yeltsin's 35 percent, and in the second round Zyuganov received 30 million votes, 40 percent of those cast. While Yeltsin won a resounding victory in that round with almost 54 percent of the vote, the discontent reflected by the substantial vote for Zyuganov cannot be ignored by policymakers or political advisers.[2] Though elderly and rural dwellers account for a disproportionate share of his support, workers, especially the older and less educated ones and those in declining industrial sectors, also form part of his constituency.

Trade unions are obviously no panacea for Russia's economic and social problems, but they do constitute the kind of intermediate organization that gives large, dispersed societal groups some collective influence over policymaking and the conditions of their lives and work. Stronger, more effective unions could mitigate the costs of reform for workers, distribute those costs more evenly, provide oversight for a more transparent and less corrupt privatization process, and press for an adequate social safety net. Workers who felt they had some voice in the reform process might be less given to its radical rejection, and thus to the support of parties that promise a return to the past. Halting reforms cannot solve the deep, systemic problems of Russia's economy. Building more effective bargaining institutions for the labor force on the other hand may make the distress caused by those reforms more palatable.

Why have Russia's unions remained weak defenders of workers' interests despite the promising beginnings of the free labor movement and the extension of democratic and legal rights? There are three central reasons:

First, those seeking to establish new, democratic unions face a daunting range of obstacles. They often want for the most basic materials, communications facilities, and information about democratic organizing methods, collective bargaining, and the like. They must attract members away from the FNPR, which remains entrenched in most enterprises and resists intrusion into its institutional space. Many face hostile managements, are isolated from other new unions, and lack the knowledge and resources to defend their rights. A general mood of demoralization pervades the labor force. As a result, initiative groups and incipient organizing efforts have often simply collapsed. New, independent, national-level unions have successfully established themselves in a few sectors, mainly energy and transportation, and one major interbranch union draws affiliates from a spectrum of manufacturing and white-collar sectors. These unions generally favor the transition to a market economy and the adoption of a Western system of worker-management bargaining. All have had limited success in recruiting members and defending their interests and incomes, and all continue to experience resource constraints and a variety of internal organizational and leadership problems.

Second, the Communist successor union, the FNPR, has generally failed to adapt to either political or economic reform. It concentrates on protecting inherited resources and prerogatives that tie most workers to formal membership but give the union little authority. There have been some limited efforts at internal democratization, but the Federation remains largely bureaucratic and hierarchical. At the national level the FNPR does press for workers' income maintenance and extension of the social safety net, and it has become more activist in response to the wage arrears crisis. But its approach to economic transition has been largely resistant and backward looking, calling for continued subsidies and state initiatives to revive production. Like its Communist predecessor the Federation cooperates closely with managers, on whom it relies for many of the benefits it distributes to members. But reform has gone forward despite the FNPR's resistance, many managers have taken advantage, and they are therefore less interested than formerly in cooperating with the union. Many FNPR unions have found themselves marginalized in the process of enterprise privatization, their distributive functions reduced and their membership declining.

Third, the weakness of the rule of law in Russian tradition and practice undercuts the effectiveness of unions. Unions are representative and bargaining agents that require civil protections of their rights and a system of enforceable contract law. Because of Russia's weak legal heritage, those in authority often feel little obligation to comply with the law or to respect the binding nature of contracts and agreements. Such lack of compliance extends to both management and government, which violate their agreements with labor so frequently that this has become the accepted norm. It is now common, for example, that workers will strike over wage arrears, reach an agreement on a schedule for repayment, and immediately set a date to renew the strike in the event that the agreement is not fulfilled. Unions are thus required to strike repeatedly in order to make good on the same demand, rendering them nearly powerless to deliver anything to their members. Such disregard for contractual norms, added to the routine violations of the rights to organize and engage in collective bargaining, creates a hostile environment for union development.

How can Russia's trade unions be strengthened? First, democracy assistance programs could provide resources and skills to the new independent unions and to activists who try to expand this movement. Russia lacks any history of democratic unionism; therefore, the transfer of skills in basic organizing, bargaining, and lobbying from experienced unionists can be extremely valuable. The new unions also need office supplies and communications equipment, and especially access to legal and technical expertise. With inadequate funding from membership dues and multiple obstacles to overcome, many will not survive unaided. Second, both the Russian government and assistance programs could pressure and encourage the FNPR to democratize, by legislative changes that weaken its inherited monopoly and through support for any internal reformist tendencies. Many observers remain pessimistic about the prospects for change in the Federation, but a few branches have moved in a democratic direction and others may follow.

WESTERN ASSISTANCE TO RUSSIA'S TRADE UNIONS

Western governmental and labor organizations can aid the development of Russia's trade unions, and in fact a number are already doing so. They include the International Labor Organization (ILO), the International Confederation of Free Trade Unions (ICFTU), Germany's Friedrich Ebert Institute, and the AFL-CIO's Free Trade Union Institute (FTUI). The major American aid initiative has been carried out by FTUI, a nonprofit organization founded in 1977 to administer grants and programs in support of democratic trade unions abroad. FTUI's work in Eastern Europe began during the 1980s, when it provided support to Solidarity during that union's struggle with the Polish Communist government. It then sought contact with emerging independent unions across the region as Communist governments collapsed. In 1990, representatives of FTUI and the United Mine Workers met with Russian miners who were just then establishing the first major independent union, the NPG. Over the following four years, these contacts grew into a multifaceted assistance program designed to help the independent unions expand their membership, strengthen their internal organization, and increase their legal rights and bargaining powers, as well as to promote contacts and cooperation among them and boost their general visibility and political influence. FTUI's efforts have been directed only toward unions that it considers both democratic and independent of management; it generally does not work with

FNPR member unions. According to a 1996 General Accounting Office report, "FTUI believes it is more effective to build new union structures rather than attempt to reform the old official unions," as these remain under the control of enterprise managers.[3]

FTUI's programs in Russia are funded by the National Endowment for Democracy (NED), of which FTUI is one of the four core grantees, and the Agency for International Development's Democracy and Governance Program. Levels of financing have been modest, beginning with a $300,000 NED grant in 1990 and increasing to a total of $2–3 million annually in combined AID and NED moneys during the program's peak funding years of 1994 and 1995. In 1995 NED funding began to decrease and in 1996 allocations from both NED and AID were reduced by some 50 percent. (Overall levels of funding from 1990 to the present are shown in Table 5.1, page 82.)

At the height of its funding in 1994–95, FTUI's program had six major components:[4]

1. A Moscow field office and four regional, one-person liaison offices in St. Petersburg, Ekaterinburg, Kemerovo, and Voronezh that provided coordination and oversight for all programs and outreach to FTUI's Russian partner unions;

2. A "Rule of Law" Project with offices in three cities that provided legal consultations and litigation in defense of trade union and worker rights, as well as advice on policy advocacy and publications to inform activists of developments in labor legislation;

3. A training program designed to transfer to Russian unionists and activists basic organizing, communications, union-building, and collective bargaining skills;

4. An Organizers' and Interns' Program that paid the salaries of trained union organizers while they served on the staffs of established unions or worked on recruitment campaigns;

5. The Russian-American Foundation for Trade Union Research and Education (RAFTURE), which produced and disseminated research on a range of topics related to trade union work while it sought to build links between unions and Russian intellectuals;

6. Communications and media projects to facilitate contacts among often isolated new unions and organizers, including direct grants of

computers and other equipment to unions as well as sponsor-
ship of radio and television programming and a weekly newspaper, *Delo.*

The program has been run by a staff of five (now four) Americans
resident in Moscow who oversee and coordinate all projects: a country
director and deputy director, a financial manager, an educational director, a director for the Organizers' and Interns' Program, and at some
times a director for a special subgrant (such as the one to the American
Federation of Teachers discussed below). The other approximately one
hundred positions have been filled by Russians as employees, contrac-
tors, or subgrantees. Many of FTUI's training seminars and other programs are run on a regional basis. More than two thousand unionists
and activists have attended training seminars, and hundreds more have
been in contact with other FTUI-sponsored programs.[5] Some components of the program were eliminated or consolidated in 1996 because of
budget cuts, and current staffing levels are considerably lower than those
cited above. A few individual American unions, including the United
Mine Workers (UMW) and the American Federation of Teachers (AFT),
have sponsored separate programs to aid their Russian counterparts, but
the major, sustained American effort has been carried on by FTUI. The
projects make limited use of American consultants and occasionally send
groups of Russian unionists to the United States for training seminars at
the George Meany Center for Labor Studies, but FTUI spends most of its
resources training and supporting Russian trade unionists on the
ground.[6]

How has this aid been received in Russia? Interviews with leaders
and activists from Russia's independent trade unions attest that most
have found American assistance valuable, especially when it gives them
concrete skills, information, and access to legal expertise.[7] At the same
time, the limitations of the program and of its impact must be recognized. The amounts of money and personnel committed have been modest from the beginning and are, as noted, shrinking substantially. Though
FTUI has been of significant benefit to new unions, most informed
observers agree that these unions are barely expanding. U.S. policymakers have also questioned the effectiveness of some of FTUI's programs,
while Russian critics claim that it deepens the dependence of Russian
unions on aid dollars and promotes divisions within the labor movement. Chapter 5 will give more consideration to these issues, as well as
examining other Western aid programs.

THE U.S. INTEREST

Why should the United States aid development of Russia's trade unions? After all, levels of unionization are low in this country and some other Western nations, which nevertheless survive as democracies. Aid money is scarce, and it is arguably being made to work at cross-purposes if it supports the building of stronger unions that then slow or resist economic reform programs the United States promotes.[8] In fact, the United States has a strong interest in supporting Russian unions because they can contribute not only to democratic stabilization but also to the success of economic reform in Russia.

Union development matters more in Russia than in the West for three reasons. First, Western states have a dense network of civic, professional, and other organizations that represent societal interests in the polity. Russia does not, and further building of democratic unions would strengthen a very weak civil society. Second, a broad range of legal, regulatory, contractual, and other protections apply to nonunionized as well as unionized workers in the West; in Russia such safeguards are absent or very weak, and are likely to be put into place only with strong pressure from organized labor. Third, the Russian economy is going through a wrenching economic transition beside which current Western recessions pale. The discontent resulting from declining real wages and poverty may lead to large-scale strike movements and civil disturbances, though levels of unrest have remained low even in the hardest-hit regions and sectors. What seems more likely is continued rejection of reform by large numbers of disaffected voters at the ballot box.

The depth of disaffection in Russian society threatens not only economic reform but possibly democracy. Recent legislative elections have constituted defeats for political moderation as well as fiscal discipline and industrial reorganization. Centrist parties have performed poorly, with voting patterns increasingly reflecting a division between pro- and antiestablishment groups, reform's winners and losers. Such polarization is risky for democracy because it increases the stakes in the political game and the threat of open conflict. Those with much invested in the current reform fear that a Communist victory would cost them everything, leading some to press for a prettified authoritarianism. Frequent suggestions during the recent presidential campaign that the election might be canceled or falsified reflected these risks.[9] Alternatively, the antiestablishment vote might bring to power a Communist or nationalist party that would threaten existing property relations within Russian society or Russia's borders with neighboring states. Such outcomes threaten instability and possibly violence in the former Soviet Union, and while Yeltsin's recent presidential reelection victory is reassuring, the electorate remains deeply divided. Stronger trade unions might prove an antidote to such polarization, conceivably forming a base for more moderate social-democratic parties on the model of their European counterparts. It is certainly in the U.S. interest to help build such institutions.

As to the apprehension about stronger unions slowing reform, even the most promarket unions will resist austerity policies and make claims on government moneys to cushion the impact on their members. But in the Russian case unions are likely at most to succeed only in moderating some reform policies; in any possible scenario they will be too weak to mount the kinds of mass resistance seen, for example, in India and Brazil.[10] Precisely such moderation may make the costs tolerable to workers, producing a slower but more certain reform process. Moreover, some analysts argue that effective collective bargaining and enforceable contracts will aid the reform process by ending the current chaos in industry, forcing managers either to pay or to lay off workers, thereby improving the effectiveness of the labor market and facilitating employment restructuring.[11] Finally, effective unions can limit the kinds of managerial and official arbitrariness and abuses that have often characterized the current reform process and that may delegitimize markets entirely in the eyes of many Russian citizens. Corrupt privatization deals, large income disparities, and masses of unpaid Russian workers do not serve the U.S. interest in promoting democracy and reform. Unions that can negotiate the price of reform for their members and keep managers honest do serve that interest. Russia is very far from having such unions, and the Western effort to help build them is modest, but it is a step in the right direction.

The current study will assess the state of both independent and successor unions in the Russian Federation, the reasons for their weak influence with both government and enterprise management, their de jure and de facto legal rights, and efforts by Western organizations to aid their development and democratization.

CHAPTER 1

SUCCESSOR AND INDEPENDENT UNIONS IN THE RUSSIAN FEDERATION

UNIONS UNDER THE SOVIET REGIME

Soviet trade unions were an arm of the state. Organized in a single hierarchy from the national-level All-Union Central Council of Trade Unions (VTsSPS)) to the 700,000 primary organizations in enterprises and institutions throughout the economy, the unions incorporated 98 percent of the labor force in obligatory membership.[1] They formed part of a "troika" in each enterprise, cooperating with managers and Communist Party officials to fulfill the state economic plan and other policies. Union officials were accountable to their superiors in both VTsSPS and the party rather than to the rank and file, and their primary responsibility was to mobilize workers for production. Managers at all levels held membership in their branch union, and union functionaries were generally subordinate to the other members of the troika. These unions afforded no genuine representation to workers and gave them no rights to bargain collectively or to strike.[2] Unions did sometimes defend workers against managerial abuses, and they were involved in health and safety and a range of other issues. Apart from the union, skilled workers exercised individual bargaining power on the shop floor because of a chronic labor shortage. But workers had no right to independent collective organization or voice, and those few who tried to form unions outside the state system met with severe repression.[3]

One major function of Soviet unions was to administer and distribute a broad range of payments, social services, and goods provided to workers at their enterprises.[4] Enterprise trade union committees helped oversee determination and payment of pensions, controlled benefits from Social Insurance Funds (for sickness, disability, maternity, etc.), and established eligibility for state welfare benefits. Union representatives held passes and vouchers to free or subsidized health facilities, vacation resorts, and children's Pioneer summer camps for enterprise employees. Unions were, moreover, responsible for the construction and management of these facilities. The scope of their activities in this regard was quite broad, including thousands of hotels, sanatoria, and camps throughout the Soviet Union; in 1975, for example, the unions managed more than 11,000 Pioneer camps. Half of all Soviet children who vacationed, some 10 million, did so at one of these camps.[5] Unions were also involved in the allocation of housing managed by enterprises, around 57 percent of total state-owned housing in Russia,[6] child care places, consumer 15, foods, and other scarce goods commonly provided to employees. Unions' role in helping decide eligibility or priority for scarce goods and critical services gave them a degree of control over members, who looked to the union officials more as a source of distribution than of representation. At the same time VTsSPS unions had come to control substantial property and financial resources, which they would take with them into the post-Soviet period.

Gorbachev's democratization, the crisis and divisions within the Communist Party, and the beginnings of economic reform posed serious challenges for the VTsSPS. Glasnost exposed a lack of mass confidence in the union structure. The government had begun to tolerate labor strikes, and the unions' response was mixed and confused. The 1989 miners' strike administered a shock: the miners showed deep contempt for the old unions; government officials used them as a scapegoat for poor conditions in the coal basins; and the strike committees raised the specter of their replacement from below by a democratic labor movement. The VTsSPS's leadership moved to reform, declaring its independence from the party and state and its commitment to the defense of workers' interests. It adopted a critical stance toward Gorbachev's economic policies.[7] However superficial, this reform proved important to the union's survival. When Yeltsin banned Communist Party organizations from Russian workplaces in July, 1991, the unions stayed.[8] When the Soviet Union collapsed at the end of that year, the successor to the VTsSPS, the Federation of Independent Trade Unions of Russia (FNPR), kept its leadership, membership, resources, and organization largely intact in the newly independent Russian Federation.

"SHOCK-THERAPY" REFORM

Before the discussion moves on to trade unions in the contemporary period, a brief digression will serve to explain the central elements of market reform and its impacts on labor. In the prereform Soviet economy, the state planned all production, allocated resources, and set prices through a command-administrative system that was inflexible and inimical to innovation. By the mid-1980s that economy was nearing stagnation and harbored thousands of inefficient, technologically obsolete, and often heavily subsidized enterprises. Shortages were endemic, living standards remained quite low, prices were highly distorted, and the budget deficit was growing. The reform program, much discussed under Gorbachev but really implemented only by Yeltsin's team, was designed to solve these problems by removing the state from control of the economy and replacing it with market mechanisms and private ownership. Yeltsin and his first prime minister, Yegor Gaidar, chose to move forward rapidly with a "shock-therapy" version of reform. In January 1992 they liberalized most prices, cut the budget, and adopted austerity policies. Over the following three years a large portion of state enterprises and other assets were privatized through sale at voucher auctions. State subsidies to most sectors were cut,[9] and the system was opened up to domestic and foreign competition. Though reform policies have been carried out inconsistently and the transition to a true market system remains far from complete, the changes have been dramatic. Their consequences for many workers, though, have been devastating.

For all its faults the old Soviet economy provided workers with social and economic security, including stable wages and prices and full employment. Shock therapy ended all of that. The January 1992 liberalization produced an immediate and massive increase in the prices of most consumer goods. As Figure 1.1 (see page 14) shows, real wages declined precipitously in that single month and remained well below their prereform (1985) level in ensuing years.[10] They declined even further, to less than 60 percent of their 1985 level, for the first three quarters of 1995, before picking up slightly by mid 1996.[11] Inflation, averaging more than 20 percent per month through 1992 and 1993—sustained but lower thereafter—wiped out savings and produced a pervasive sense of economic insecurity. (See Figure 1.2, page 14). The minimum wage fell to a fraction of the subsistence level (see Table 1.1, page 15), and by the fall of 1994, 23.6 percent of all employees had wage income below that level. While none depend exclusively on job earnings, large numbers of workers on the lower rungs of the salary scale have found themselves among the 25–30 percent of the population living in poverty (see Table 1.2, page 15).[12] Many enterprises, affected by massive economic disruptions as well as subsidy cuts, began paying even these skimpy wages late or not at all, and wage arrears have mounted to crisis proportions. Already in November 1994 nearly half of all enterprises were in arrears on payroll, and the majority of workers were not receiving their full

FIGURE 1.1
THE REAL AVERAGE WAGE, 1991–96 (1985=100)

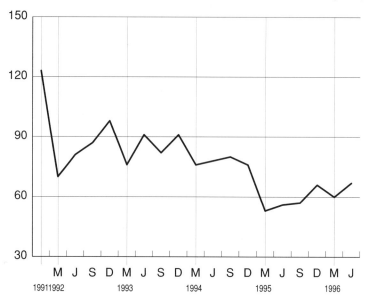

Source: Data for 1992 are from *Russian Economic Trends (RET)* 2, no. 3 (London: Whurr Publishers, 1993), Table 23, p. 32; for 1993 and 1994, from *RET* 3, no. 4 (1994), Table 37, pp. 46–47; for 1995, from *RET* 5, no. 1 (1996), Table 42, p. 52; and for 1991 and 1996, *RET* 5, no. 2 (1996), Table 43, p. 62.

FIGURE 1.2
MONTHLY INFLATION (CPI), 1992–96

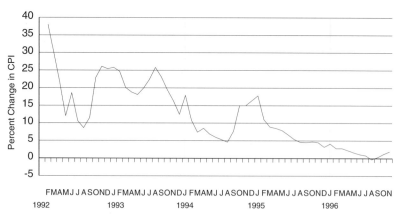

Source: Russian Economic Trends, Monthly Update, April 22, 1996, Statistical Annex, Table 1 (no page); ibid., December 16, 1996, Table 1, p. 16.

TABLE 1.1
MINIMUM WAGE AND SUBSISTENCE MINIMUM IN RUSSIA, 1992–95 (in rubles)

	Jan. 1992	Jan. 1993	Jan. 1994	1995 Average
Minimum Wage	342	900	14,620	42,621
Subsistence Minimum	635	5,547	47,189	264,100

Source: Data for 1992–94, furnished by Goskomstat, the Russian state statistical committee, are adapted from Tatyana Chetvernina, "Minimum Wages in Russia: Fantasy Chasing Fact," in Guy Standing and Daniel Vaughal-Whitehead, *Minimum Wages in Central and Eastern Europe: From Protection to Destitution* (New York: Central European University Press, 1995), Table 3-5, pp. 61–62; data for 1995 are from *Russian Economic Trends**4, no. 4 (London: Whurr Publishers, 1995): 55.

TABLE 1.2
SHARE OF THE RUSSIAN FEDERATION POPULATION WITH INCOMES BELOW THE SUBSISTENCE LEVEL

1992 . . . . .34%

1993 . . . . .32%

1994 . . . . .24%

1995 . . . . .25%

1996 (January–August) 23%

Source: Russian Economic Trends, Monthly Update, November 18, 1996, p. iv.

* *Russian Economic Trends* is produced by the Working Centre for Economic Reform, Government of the Russian Federation, with the assistance of the London School of Economics' Centre for Economic Performance team working within the Russian European Centre for Economic Policy. We thank them for permission to use this data in this book.

wages on time; in the first half of 1996, 75 percent of the total national monthly wage bill was overdue.[13] Real income has not fallen as much as wages, and indeterminate numbers of workers are supplementing their pay with earnings in the gray economy or small, private ventures, but the overall downward pressure on living standards has been great. Large-scale rent seeking (such as monopoly pricing) and corruption contribute to growing income disparities.

Reform has also generated unemployment. Industrial production has declined by half since 1989, and large numbers of enterprises are in a highly precarious state. They have begun to lay off workers, especially since mid-1993, with a simultaneous decline in vacancies (see Figure 1.3). Though the official rate of unemployment—9 percent at the end of 1996—remains low by international standards, it excludes an epidemic of "hidden unemployment" among workers whose enterprises have stopped production for periods of time, reduced them to part-time work, or sent them on involuntary leaves with little or no pay. According to official statistics some 4–5 percent of the population is affected overall, producing an overall rate of about 13

FIGURE 1.3
UNEMPLOYED (THOUSANDS)

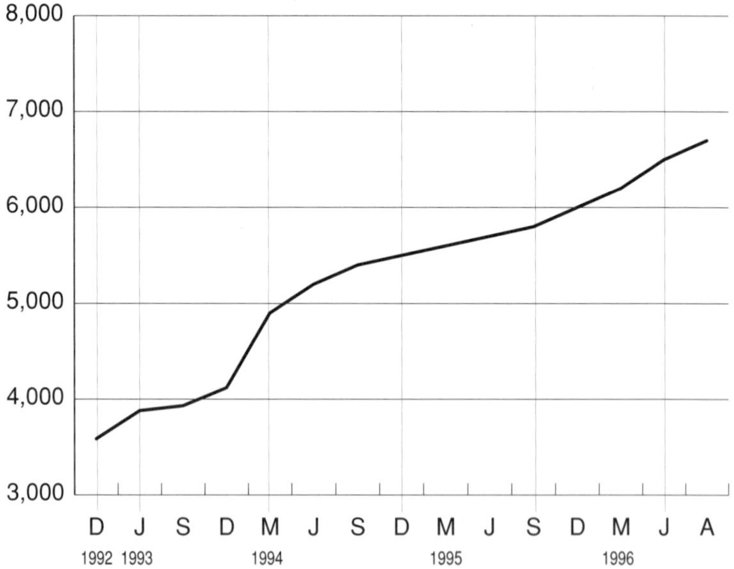

Source: Jan Vanous, ed., *PlanEcon Report: Developments in the Economies of Eastern Europe and the Former USSR* 12, nos. 1–2 (January 31, 1996), p. 20; nos. 33–36 (October 14, 1996), p. 14.

percent unemployed and underemployed. Official rates are understated, and some estimates are considerably higher; an ILO study by Guy Standing estimated "hidden" (or suppressed) unemployment in the hard-hit industrial sector at 35 percent of the workforce already in 1994.[14] The social safety net for workers who lose their jobs is developing but remains weak and porous. Unemployment benefits are very low and difficult to obtain, and only a minority collect.[15] Labor market institutions are poorly developed, and the Federal Employment Service is ill-equipped to help the displaced find new jobs. Yeltsin recently fired its chair, Fyodor Prokopov, for inefficiency.[16] Survey research shows that fear of unemployment is widespread and growing.[17] Perhaps most seriously, some unemployed workers are cut off from the network of enterprise-based social services. At the same time, many who produce little or nothing remain at their enterprises and retain enterprise-owned housing and other services. This is one factor helping to stabilize the situation at least for the time being. It is in such an atmosphere of depressed and unpaid wages, rising unemployment, and pervasive insecurity that Russia's trade unions must work.

Trade Unions in the Reform Period: FNPR, the Communist Successor

The Communist successor umbrella union, the FNPR (Federation of Independent Trade Unions) has proved resilient, using its inherited resources and advantages to maintain its dominant position as the representative of Russian labor in the reform period. It came out of the Communist era with a Russia-wide structure of committees extending from the center down to the individual factory or place of work, uniting twenty-nine production branch unions (classified by industry type) and seventy-seven regional interbranch organizations.[18] The Federation retained its predecessor's membership roles and dues (withheld automatically from payroll), claiming in 1992 to represent more than 60 million of the 73 million members of Russia's labor force.[19] FNPR cadres entrenched themselves in Russian enterprises, where they continued a close working relationship with managers, who also remained a presence within union ranks. The Federation suffers from extremely weak authority and legitimacy among rank-and-file members, a legacy of both its predecessor's subordination to the party-state during the Communist period and its bureaucratic working style. Repeated attitude surveys have attested to workers' low levels of confidence in the FNPR. A 1993 survey, for example, showed that only 23 percent of polled workers believed the trade unions at their enterprise could defend their interests, while a later poll showed some 90 percent of FNPR members dissatisfied and one at the end of 1996 showed that only 7 percent of the population fully trusted trade unions.[20] Federation leaders themselves periodically lament the faint level of workers' confidence in the organization.

Most members nevertheless stay because the union provides goods and services (time at vacation resorts, consumer goods), because many believe their access to social insurance funds depends on membership, and because of inertia and lack of alternatives. Labor specialist Victor Komarovsky observed in 1992 that, though a proper reregistration and voluntary dues collection would no doubt shrink the ranks of the FNPR, "many fear parting ways with the old trade unions, though they are discredited as part of the administrative-bureaucratic apparatus, because they still can influence the situation, and the new unions, even the miners, lack the strength and authority to tip the scales of confidence in their direction," and this remains true today.[21] Some who do wish to leave for newly formed alternative unions claim intimidation by FNPR cadres, including threats that they will be denied factory-based benefits and services, and fear harassment and discrimination in job assignments by pro-FNPR enterprise managers.[22] The FNPR's membership has nevertheless declined over the past four years because of the breakaway of groups to form or join independent unions, the splitting off of constituent branch unions, movement of labor into the largely nonunion private sector, and members' disaffection.

The FNPR's low authority among the rank and file has led to relatively weak mobilizational capacities. Evidence is strong that the union has, until recently, been able neither to organize sustained strikes nor prevent or control those that arose from below. Its periodically threatened national strikes have materialized mostly as single-day affairs. Such brief and symbolic protests are insufficient to pressure the government into meeting FNPR demands. Its weak leadership has helped undermine the FNPR's claim to represent the vast majority of Russia's workers and damaged its effectiveness as a bargaining agent for labor. Recently, however, with the deterioration of workers' conditions headlined by the wage arrears crisis, FNPR-sponsored protests have grown larger, bringing out several hundred thousand workers in semiannual, nationwide demonstrations, and the union has grown more militant in some sectors, particularly coal mining.[23] More important, it remains the only union functioning across the length and breadth of the Russian Federation, as well as the only union available to speak for workers in most sectors of Russia's economy.

THE FNPR'S POLICY AGENDAS

The FNPR has sought to resist or limit many aspects of the country's economic reform program in the process of defending the incomes and jobs of its members. It has defined its constituency broadly to include not only workers but pensioners, students, and recipients of state transfer payments generally. Much of the Federation's energies have concentrated on maintaining the value of what its clients receive in the face of price liberalization and inflation: it has pressed for state guarantees of a minimum wage equivalent to the subsistence minimum; it has persistently demanded indexation of wages, pensions, stipends, incomes, and savings to inflation; and it has insisted on selective price controls over essential goods and energy.[24] In the earlier stages of reform FNPR unions advocated the continuation of state subsidies, soft credits, and conversion funds to preserve jobs at failing enterprises. Having largely lost these battles, unions demanded unemployment compensation and state guarantees of retraining and rehiring elsewhere for those who are displaced, while they still insisted that the state must shore up production. In response to the government's plans to privatize state-owned businesses and enterprises, the FNPR demanded that workers should have the right to acquire a controlling share of the enterprises at which they were employed.[25] And though, as Chapter 4 will show, these demands were partially met, the Federation has remained critical of abuses and the lack of transparency in the privatization process. With the emergence of the crisis of arrears, the FNPR has concentrated its demands on full payment of back wages and governmental debts to industry and to public sector workers. It has also demanded that the government stop the ongoing decline of production by lowering taxes and adopting protectionist policies. Various branch unions of the FNPR, especially those involved in defense and energy, have put forth their own demands, which usually complement those of the Federation but not always; there are episodes of conflict, as when energy sector workers press for world market energy prices while the leadership supports domestic price controls.[26]

Overall, the FNPR has attempted to defend workers' interests but with a largely conservative agenda, one that resists most aspects of economic reform and insists on continuing state responsibility for both living standards and production. The union has made little adaptation to the emerging market features of Russia's economy, ignoring governmental reformers' insistence that workers' demands must now be resolved at the factory level.[27] Moreover, many of the FNPR's wage and income demands have contributed to inflation (as have those of the independent unions):

real wages stagnate as prices keep pace with the rapid rise in nominal wages and incomes. The continuation of state subsidies and credits likewise provides no resolution of industry's deep structural problems. Some of the FNPR's policies are more adaptive. It has, for example, contributed to the creation of the modest safety net for unemployed workers, including temporary compensation and the beginnings of a job referral network, which is broadly seen as necessary to ease the transition to a functional labor market. Moreover, some of the groups it defends, such as pensioners, cannot be expected to adjust and must rely on the state for support. Basically, though, the union has engaged in piecemeal resistance to a reform program for which it has no coherent alternative, and it has therefore lost more than it has won on most issues. Its successes have been modest and temporary, and the situation of workers has continued to deteriorate.

RELATIONS WITH GOVERNMENT AND MANAGERIAL ELITES

The FNPR's activities and influence-seeking strategies have from the outset been heavily oriented toward governmental and managerial elites. In the fall of 1991, as the independent Russian state was becoming established, Yeltsin offered the unions—both FNPR and independents—a "social partnership" with government. Mindful that mass strikes by miners and other workers had played a significant role in the downfall of Gorbachev, Yeltsin was seeking to create bargaining and conciliation mechanisms that would assure labor peace. The social partnership was shortly institutionalized in the Tripartite Commission for the Regulation of Social and Labor Relations, which brought together representatives of government, industry, and labor to negotiate an annual general agreement on social and economic policy, very much along the lines of similar commissions in a number of Western European countries. The FNPR agreed to the role of a "constructive opposition" and was granted the dominant place (nine of fourteen seats) as labor's representative on the 1992 commission.[28] The government thus essentially recognized the FNPR as the bargaining agent for much of Russia's labor force, shoring up the union's status and claims to legitimacy. Despite serious problems with both the structure and functioning of the Tripartite Commission (to be discussed further in Chapter 3), defections from it by both union and government representatives, and periodic threats by the union to resort to mass protests and strikes in order to force the government's hand, the FNPR has focused considerable energies on the Tripartite Commission, returning again and again to the bargaining table.

The FNPR has also sought actively to influence policymaking in the Russian legislature, both the old Supreme Soviet (1991–93, when it was forcibly dissolved by Yeltsin) and the Duma (January 1994–present), developing legislative agendas, preparing draft resolutions and documents, and cultivating contacts with sympathetic deputies on relevant committees. Interviews with ranking members of Supreme Soviet committees in mid-1993 presented a picture of the FNPR regularly consulting and somewhat successfully lobbying on income and social welfare issues,[29] as well as privatization policy and trade union rights. While the union's influence in the present Duma is less clear, it continues to speak out on legislative issues. The FNPR also maintains visibility through publication of a national newspaper, *Rabochaya Tribuna* (Workers' Tribune), which is widely seen as its mouthpiece, and through the activities of its chairmen, Igor Klochkov (until his resignation in October 1993) and his successor, Mikhail Shmakov, who act as self-appointed national spokesmen for labor.

The FNPR has made its strongest alliances with managers, both at the enterprise level and in national politics. In 1992 it joined with Arkady Volsky's Russian Union of Industrialists and Entrepreneurs and the broader centrist political alliance, Civic Union, to help bring down the pro-shock therapy Gaidar government. Its cooperation with managerial organizations continued in the Tripartite Commission, and in the ill-fated party grouping Trade Unions and Industrialists of Russia/Union of Labor bloc that gained only 1.5 percent of the vote and failed to win any seats in the December 1995 Duma election.[30] While such union-management alliances may make little sense in the context of a Western market economy, the structure of interests differs significantly in a state-controlled economy such as Russia had in 1992 (and to a decreasing but considerable extent still has). In that setting, labor and managers share an interest in pressuring the state for allocations, subsidies, soft credits, and other concessions, and there is a logic in their cooperating against austerity budgets and stabilization policies. One analyst even suggests that FNPR unions should be seen as representing not the interests of workers but, along with managers, the interests of their production branch.[31] Of course, the FNPR's leadership is adept at such alliances because union and management cadre have worked closely together for decades and share a heritage of socialization in the Soviet industrial bureaucracy. The FNPR is in general much more comfortable with and capable of elite-level bargaining with either government or managers than it is in regard to grassroots organizing or building rapport with the rank and file. With the progress of reform, however, the union-management alliance has become increasingly strained. The state's reduction of subsidies and soft credits to most sectors of the economy has limited the potential gains of joint lobbying, though the massive coal and agricultural sectors remain heavily subsidized. Many managers of privatized enterprises have lost interest in cooperation with unions, a point to which Chapter 4 will return.

DEVELOPMENTS WEAKENING THE FNPR

While the FNPR remains by far dominant among unions in the Russian Federation, a number of internal and external developments have tended to weaken it. It has lost millions of members, experienced divisions and defections over reform policy, and demonstrated a growing lack of unity. Though the leadership continues to claim some 50 million of the original 60 million members, informed observers place current membership below 40 million, and independent studies confirm a decline of some 25 percent.[32] Several constituent unions have broken away in part or in whole, most significantly the 2 million-strong Trade Union of the Mining and Metallurgical Industry, which split from the FNPR in 1992 to support Gaidar's reform program and gain more control over the branch union's resources. The large Moscow regional affiliate of the Federation has pursued independent alliances with a variety of small socialist parties, while several other regional unions have bypassed the central leadership to form independent ties with parties across the political spectrum.[33] In any case the FNPR has minimal influence over its members' votes, as evidenced by the abysmal performance of the party-management bloc in the 1995 parliamentary elections.

Both the government and the independent unions have challenged the FNPR's property ownership, control over Social Insurance Funds (SIF), and other prerogatives. There have been proposals to nationalize union property—periodic reports indicate that some properties have been seized by regional governments—and independents have asserted rights to proportionate shares.[34] The pension fund had been transferred to state control in 1990. In the fall of 1993, when the FNPR openly opposed Yeltsin's dissolution of the parliament, the president retaliated by attacking its resource base. A governmental decree prohibited enterprises' financial organs from collecting trade union dues, in effect eliminating the automatic dues checkoff for FNPR members. A second decree transferred control of the critical Social Insurance Fund to the state, to be run "with the participation of the trade unions."[35] There are conflicting reports as to whether these decrees have been implemented, but a state management board for SIF has been established and FNPR control has at least been reduced. Finally, privatized enterprises are beginning to offer less to their employees, spinning off expensive social services or transferring them to municipalities.[36] In sum, the FNPR's financial and resource base has eroded. It has less to distribute to its members, and they have commensurately less incentive to stay.

Potential for Democratization of the FNPR

Can the FNPR democratize? Critics charge that the Federation lacks both the inclination and incentive to represent workers genuinely or to struggle in their defense, and that it is a wealthy, self-serving, and venal bureaucracy interested mainly in preserving its property and prerogatives. According to this view, at the enterprise level union officials cooperate with and back managers in order to keep their offices, cars, and other privileges. At the national level, as noted, the organization controls substantial wealth and property, and charges of corruption and misuse of funds are common. In 1993 the union-administered Social Insurance Funds, financed from payroll taxes, amounted to 215 billion rubles; a 1992 Supreme Soviet investigation had found that such moneys were being used to finance union officials' salaries and were diverted into banking structures.[37] Even if it loses members and control over SIF, moreover, the union would retain the bulk of its revenues because reform has allowed it to put many of its assets, including vacation resorts and sanitoria, to commercial use. A substantial though indeterminate part of its income derives from profits on such recreational and other properties.[38]

Though there is some truth to this characterization, the Federation's position seems more complicated and its potential for reform greater. The FNPR does seek to build legitimacy among members, both by fighting government policies detrimental to labor and by continuing to exercise its patronage powers at the enterprise level. But the union cannot take a strongly confrontational stance against government because it fears further loss of status and control: the government could decree a reregistration of membership, as has been done in some other post-Communist countries, or carry out the threatened transfer of its property to the state.[39] The union likewise depends on management for the goods and services it distributes to members, and these could be jeopardized by hard bargaining. Thus, the FNPR is in a double bind, trying to retain members by promoting their interests without antagonizing government or management.[40] This bind is becoming tighter as the situation of many workers deteriorates, membership declines, the FNPR's middleman role evaporates, managers lose interest in allying with it, and the independents demonstrate that unions can defend workers' interests more aggressively. In response some branches of the FNPR have become more militant in the campaign against wage arrears and in their recent leadership of strikes. One scholar who spent time in the Kuzbass studying the FNPR's Trade Union of Coal Industry Workers found that some mine unions had begun to defend workers against, for example, pay inequities and managers' efforts to extend working hours, and that all insisted they would resist mine closings and redundancies unless a comprehensive reemployment program was in place. She concluded that there are grounds for hope that the unions can reform. Officials from both the International Labor Organization (ILO) and the International Confederation of Free Trade Unions (ICFTU), who have worked extensively with Russian unions, believe that there are significant pressures for reform within the FNPR.[41] The potential for democratization, at least of some FNPR unions, should be taken seriously.

TRADE UNIONS IN THE REFORM PERIOD: THE INDEPENDENT UNIONS

The independents, mostly founded in 1991 and 1992, are the other important group of trade unions in Russia. Some are genuine products of Gorbachev's democratization; their leaders emerged spontaneously, often from strike committees, and gained authority among the rank and file by challenging and repudiating the old statist power structure—management, government, and the old trade unions. Others broke away from the FNPR to move in more democratic and proreform directions, asserting their independence from management and becoming more accountable to their members. The independents are much closer than the FNPR to the Western model of trade unions.[42] They see themselves as representing exclusively the interests of workers. They seek genuine collective bargaining, are quite willing to take an adversarial attitude toward management, and are able to organize collective action. Most members join voluntarily, and leaders are accountable through election. In sectors where they are established, the independents' demonstration effect exerts pressure on FNPR unions to become more responsive to the interests of their own members. They serve as a somewhat flawed model of democratic institutions in a society that still has few.

At this time the independents include only a small part of the labor force and have consolidated in a limited number of sectors, mainly energy and transport. Most represent workers in a single industry or occupational group. They include the Independent Miners' Union (NPG), the Mining and Metallurgical Workers' Trade Union, the Federation of Air Traffic Controllers' Unions (FPAD), the Federation of Civil Aviation Pilots' Unions (FPALS), the Railroad Engineers', Seafarers', and Dockers' unions, and one major interbranch association, the Association of Social Trade Unions (Sotsprof). Of these only the metallurgists have a nationwide structure. Some small, unaffiliated regional and local trade union structures are also well established. Scores of additional independent unions operate in Russia, mainly loose, often ephemeral confederations or small, locally based organizations sometimes affiliated with political parties or movements.[43] Most have little influence or significance beyond a small circle. Organizing initiatives have reportedly remained widespread throughout Russia's labor force but have failed to produce important new unions.[44] At present, total membership in independent unions is approximately 3 million, and growth since 1992 has been modest at best (see Table 1.3). If the 2 million members of the Mining and Metallurgical Workers' Trade Union

TABLE 1.3
MEMBERSHIP IN MAJOR INDEPENDENT UNIONS

	1992	1996
Sotsprof	250,000	500,000 (150,000)
Miners (NPG)	70,000	95,000 (75,000)
Air Traffic Controllers (FPAD)	5,000	10,000
Pilots (FPALS)	30,000	25,000
Railroad Engineers	2,000	6,000
Metallurgists	2,000,000	2,000,000
Seafarers	n.a.	50,000
Dockers	n.a.	20,000 (est.)

Sources: Figures for 1992 are from Valentin Rupets, "Trade Union Movement in 'Post-Totalitarian Russia,' (classification essay)," *New Labor Movement* (informational and analytical bulletin), nos. 3–4, Moscow, 1992, p. 44, and are reported by the unions themselves. Figures for 1996 are from Scott Reynolds, former executive director of the Moscow Office of FTUI, in a telephone interview with the author, June 27, 1996, and are also reported by the unions; figures in parentheses are Reynolds's more realistic estimates.

and others that broke away en masse from the FNPR are excluded, the numbers of those that have mobilized from the ground up are in the hundreds of thousands. Many organizing drives founder because of a lack of resources, inexperienced leadership, obstruction by management and the old unions, and mass exhaustion and disillusionment. Those unions that do gain firm footing must still compete with the FNPR, though they have little in the way of tangible offerings to distribute to their members, and must often fight a war of attrition with management.[45]

Before discussing the individual unions, it pays to consider why independents have developed strongly in mining, metallurgy, and transport but not in most other branches of the economy. Several characteristics distinguish the sectors that have produced independents. First, miners everywhere display high levels of solidarity and militancy, arguably because of the nature and danger of the labor process in which they are engaged. Second, most independents represent labor forces with relatively high levels of education.[46] Third, most produce goods and services that are vital to the economy, putting them in a better strategic bargaining position than other workers; threats to withhold fuel or transport must be taken seriously. Finally, workers in these fields initially saw some prospect of benefiting from reform because of the apparent hard currency earning potential—coal and metallurgical workers believed they could sell their products abroad; pilots and air traffic controllers realized the airlines earned foreign exchange from international passengers and landing rights. Such real or perceived advantages pushed workers in these sectors to form new unions or to break with the nonmilitant, antireform FNPR. Throughout postsocialist Eastern Europe independent unions have formed in these same occupational sectors, indicating that structural factors are important determinants of the tendency to organize independently, and that the spread of independent unions to other job categories will be more difficult.

THE INDEPENDENTS' STRUCTURE AND LEADERSHIP

Sotsprof, the largest of the newly formed independents, is in many respects unique. It is a national interbranch association established in its present form in February 1991, under the chairmanship of Sergei Khramov, and originally closely allied with a social-democratic party. It invites affiliation by groups or workers that have organized on their own in any sector of the economy and performs the critical role of registering these groups as legal unions. Though Sotsprof's claim of 500,000 members is considered highly exaggerated by informed observers (see Table

1.3, page 25), its affiliates include medical personnel, engineering and scientific workers, metalworkers, transport workers, and builders, and it is the only established alternative to the FNPR in many such sectors. It is committed to "responsible" unionism and collective bargaining, and unlike the other independents it sees strikes as a last resort. Sotsprof has been the most aggressive of the independents in challenging the FNPR, not only by providing an alternative national organizational umbrella but by demanding a share in the Federation's property and creating separate social security schemes for its members. Khramov has urged the government to "rout the bosses" of the old union.[47] At the same time, Sotsprof has a number of internal problems. Khramov is a controversial figure whose financing policies and leadership style have produced disputes with affiliates and charges of corruption. At least one study has concluded that local branches of Sotsprof frequently collapse because the central union fails to support them, though other observers report that the union has some vibrant regional organizations despite problems at the center.[48]

The Independent Miners' Union (NPG), which emerged out of the massive strike movement of 1989–91 under the leadership of Aleksandr Sergeev, is the most visible of the independents. Though initially accepting only miners who worked on the coal face, the NPG recently liberalized its membership rules and expanded to a claimed 95,000 members. The vast majority of workers in the mining sector, numbering more than one million, remain within the FNPR's Independent Trade Union of Coal Industry Employees.[49] Nevertheless, the NPG's authority and influence extend well beyond its membership, and it has effectively managed strikes that included large numbers of miners from outside its ranks. The most militant and strike-prone of all Russia's unions, the NPG has delivered substantial benefits to its members and other miners, including huge wage increases and government concessions on pensions, vacations, and other benefits.

The NPG also has its problems, however. The government has frequently failed to deliver on its promised concessions, while price inflation and other factors have often rendered gains ephemeral. NPG affiliates have also engaged in commercial activities in order to generate revenues that would make them more competitive with the FNPR. Such commercial activities have diverted some leaders from union building and alienated them from the rank and file. In the South Kuzbass, for example, "the NPG and the strike committees were seen to have deserted the workers, most of their leaders reputedly using the workers' movement as a stepping stone out of the mine into commerce." In response, some miners who had joined the NPG have returned to the FNPR miners' union because it still provides better benefits and because they are disillusioned with the prospect of building unions they can trust.[50]

The remaining independents are breakaways from the FNPR, including the massive Mining and Metallurgical Workers' Trade Union, led until recently by Boris Misnik, and several small unions in the transport sector. Some doubt the democratic credentials of the breakaways, particularly of the metallurgists, questioning whether the union has really established its independence from management at lower levels, but the leadership's policies have certainly moved in this direction. The transport unions have relied heavily on strikes and strike threats to press wage and other demands; the pilots' and air traffic controllers' unions are especially inclined to make chronic strike threats that hold civil aviation hostage to their demands. They have had some success in pressing their claims, but they have also experienced serious confrontations with the government over the legality of some transport strikes.

THE INDEPENDENTS' POLICIES AND POLITICS

The independent unions are proreform and promarket, favoring the end of state control and the transition to a competitive, profit-driven economy. They have been a more or less consistent source of support for the government's reform policies. Initially, as noted, the leaders of most independents believed that their sectors had substantial possibilities for exporting or earning foreign currency through services, and would therefore benefit from reform and economic independence. Those beliefs have more often than not turned out to be false. Industries such as mining and metallurgy now face continuing declines in production, plant closures, and layoffs. The independents have nevertheless retained their commitment to the market, accepting that most state subsidies must end and that shrinking and restructuring are necessary to produce efficient, profitable enterprises. They have turned back to the state mainly to demand aid in resettlement, retraining, and employment programs for those displaced. NPG chairman Sergeev fairly distinguishes his union's agenda from that of the FNPR, "The managerial [FNPR] trade unions demand money to preserve the old order, we—to bring our industry into the market."[51] Former Mining and Metallurgical Workers' chair Misnik has backtracked somewhat more from his promarket stance, pressing the state not only for employment aid but also for "moderate protectionism . . . in some cases—it is irrational to allow raw material bases to perish."[52]

The independents' proreform stance has sometimes led to a perception that their leaderships are too politicized, more concerned with supporting Yeltsin's policies than with responding to ordinary workers' concerns. Arguments about the longer-term benefits of the market are a hard sell among the unions' rank and file when wages are falling and unemployment rising, and the contradiction between the leaderships' market-oriented politics and their members' short-term interests limits their appeal. At the same time, the independents have been far more aggressive than the FNPR in organizing strikes and other industrial action to press their members' wage and other demands. As a practical matter these demands have often been directed at government, which has continued to control much of the economy in the transitional period. In the long run, though, the independents' leaders see managers as responsible for running their enterprises and collective bargaining at the company level as the central means for labor to achieve its goals in the developing market economy.

A number of limitations combine to check the potential influence of the independents. Their efforts at recruiting and retaining the rank and file remain weak because of a lack of basic organizing skills and workers' general distrust of hierarchy and organization. Though the independents have mounted an impressive effort to secure their legal rights, both in abstract principle and against the claims of the FNPR, those rights are often unenforceable. These unions could maximize their collective influence through unity, but repeated efforts at organizing a national confederation foundered. The Labor Confederation of Russia (KTR) was finally created in April 1995 and almost immediately split because of conflicts over leadership, with the NPG withdrawing and forming a second All-Russian Confederation of Labor (VKT) with Sotsprof.[53] In electoral politics as well they have divided their support among numerous parties. Finally, the independents have received a very limited payback from the government for their support not only on reform policies but at a number of critical political junctures.[54] They have sought from the government greater recognition and influence, including a larger say in labor policy and more representation on the Tripartite Commission and other governmental bodies. Instead the government has continued to give the lion's share of representation to the FNPR, ostensibly because of its numerical superiority but also because it is more controllable and less prone to strikes and militance. Yeltsin has taken the independents for granted, resulting in frustration and alienation among their leaders.

POLITICAL AND CULTURAL OBSTACLES TO UNION BUILDING

There are several additional political and cultural obstacles to union building in the Russian Federation. The socialist factory functioned very differently from its Western counterpart. In addition to providing workers with employment and wage income, the factory in the former Soviet Union provided or distributed many goods and services that would normally be provided either by the private sector at large or the welfare state in the West, typically including housing, child care, medical care, pensions and disability pay, access to recreational and vacation facilities, scarce consumer 15 and goods. Moreover, many of these benefits were distributed to workers differentially at the discretion of factory management, while access to others depended on seniority, time on waiting lists, or informal connections. The worker and his or her family thus experienced an exceptionally high degree of dependence on the factory to meet most of life's needs, and an employee often had a substantial personal investment (that is, preference or years on a waiting list) that could not be replaced outside that particular enterprise. Analysts of Russian labor's relative passivity in the postsocialist period have pointed to this pattern of multiple dependence on the enterprise as an important constraint blocking workers' organizing efforts. Workers simply have too much to lose by challenging managers. According to Stephen Crowley, for example, such dependence creates severe problems for workers in trying to mount collective action, especially in the manufacturing sector, where distribution of the traditional goods and services has been most plentiful.[55] Although enterprises' delivery of benefits has declined over the past few years, paradoxically, in the face of skyrocketing inflation and severe shortages, their capacity to continue the practice through barter arrangements has in many cases reinforced dependence.

Other inherited patterns and predispositions also tend to inhibit workers' organizing efforts. The wages and benefits available to Russian workers have long depended on decisions and bargaining between managers and state officials, with the official unions playing a subsidiary role, and many workers have continued to look to their managers to protect the labor collective in the face of rapidly changing state policies and economic conditions. Though tensions between workers and management are, and have always been, abundant, a strong element of managerial paternalism also infuses this relationship. Managers have often acted, either sincerely or manipulatively, to reinforce workers' sense of dependence and protection. The credible claim that management and workers until recently shared interests vis-à-vis the state (in gaining subsidies, credits, etc.) as well as against outsiders who might gain control over the enterprise during privatization has further discouraged conflict.[56] Managerial paternalism has declined significantly in an economy characterized by privatizations, but its tradition and psychology still have a strong influence in Russia's industrial relations.

Trade unions have developed and functioned in the West as part of a dense network of autonomous societal organizations—including professional and managerial associations, political parties, and the like—that form to represent their members' interests. Russian civil society has virtually no tradition or experience of such autonomous organizations, and many that have emerged since 1989 suffer from similar weaknesses, including inexperienced and ineffective leadership, internal divisiveness, weak membership retention, and failures to consolidate. Difficulty in building mass membership organizations, in other words, is pervasive and by no means limited to trade unions. Indeed, several of the most effective and sustained organizations and political parties, including the Communist Party of the Russian Federation and the Agrarian Party, parallel the FNPR in that they inherited organizational and resource bases from the Communist period. Independent societal organizations are now permitted in Russia, but the norms, skills, and accountability mechanisms that will allow such organizations to develop broadly are weak among workers and throughout Russian society. Organizations will develop more quickly if large numbers of Russians are exposed to democratic norms, and if the skills and accountability mechanisms are learned or transferred from societies that have long had them in place.

Recently, a group of Russian researchers suggested three scenarios for the future development of Russia's successor unions, the FNPR:

- their slow death over a long period;

- a rapid breakdown of the successor unions at the basic level and their replacement with new, independent unions;

- a cardinal reform, transforming these unions into real representatives of the interests of workers.[57]

Unless independent unions develop more rapidly, or pressures for reform within the FNPR intensify, the first scenario will likely prevail and most of Russia's labor force will be left outside any union structure.

If new independent or democratized FNPR unions are to develop in Russia, both the legal infrastructure and practice of formal bargaining and contracting between labor and management must be developed. The following chapter considers the theory and practice of trade union rights and collective action in the reform period.

CHAPTER 2

UNIONS' DE JURE AND DE FACTO RIGHTS TO ORGANIZE, BARGAIN, AND STRIKE

DEVELOPMENT OF THE LEGAL INFRASTRUCTURE AND ITS DEFICIENCIES

Since the creation of the independent Russian state in late 1991, reformers have consciously sought to bring Russian labor law into compliance with international (mainly European and American) norms by establishing legal foundations upon which unions can operate and replacing administrative forms of labor regulation with contractual ones. New legislation has given unions rights to organize, to represent their members in collective bargaining, to have grievances heard by management, to initiate mediation and arbitration of labor disputes, and, with some restrictions, to lead strikes. Before reviewing this legislation in more detail, however, it is instructive to stress some constraints that limit its effectiveness in the Russian context.

The first and most important of these is the weakness of the "rule of law"—of well-established legal norms and a functioning legal system in Russia. Throughout the Soviet period decisions were made and enforced by state and political administrators. Courts, contracts, and litigation played a relatively minor role, and both civil law generally and contract law in particular remained poorly developed.[1] As a result, in the present system most political and business figures have little respect for the law, little regard for the legally binding nature of obligations and contracts, and little expectation that these will be enforced through the courts. Further, personnel development and the institutional infrastructure necessary for a Western system of labor relations are only at the formative stage. Labor lawyers, for example, remain very scarce, and a Federal

Service for Resolving Collective Labor Disputes was established only in 1993. Thus, trade unions may engage in collective bargaining but face widespread violations of the resulting general and wage agreements by management, an inadequate system of enforcement, and lack of experience with litigation or arbitration. Instead of relying on the prescribed procedures for contract grievances, workers and trade unions frequently call for government intervention in what are essentially labor-management relations (though the government is a major violator of its own agreements with labor). In other areas as well, labor unions, managements, and government regularly flout legislation and ignore commitments that should have legal force.

The effectiveness of the new labor legislation is also qualified by the fact that the labor code, laws, and regulations have been a patchwork of old and new that is continually being changed. For most of the period under review, the basic labor code of the Russian Federation was an October 1992 revision of the Brezhnev-era code, which includes the provision "until passage of corresponding legislative acts, norms of the former USSR apply insofar as they do not contradict the Constitution and legislation of the Russian Federation."[2] This labor code has been undergoing revision since the spring of 1993 to adapt it to conditions of the developing private economy. Much other relevant legislation, including a Civil Code that establishes the basis for labor and other contracts, was until recently mired in the political process. The result has been a lack of clarity as to which laws applied—the old Soviet labor code, laws from the Gorbachev period, or legislation and decrees passed under Yeltsin. The FNPR has protested some current labor practices and Yeltsin administration decrees as violations of the social protection provisions of the 1992 labor code, but these protests have fallen on deaf ears. The murky situation has allowed for a few instances of arbitrary government action in areas not yet covered by new laws and additional difficulties in enforcing legislation when new drafts covering the same ground are already before the legislature.

Finally, the anomalous status of the FNPR and the conflicts of interest between the Federation and the new independent unions have complicated the making of labor law. One might expect that unions could agree to support measures protecting labor and trade union rights. Instead the FNPR is often at odds with the new independents over the provisions of labor legislation, the one seeking to defend its entrenched position, the others to establish their rights. Both have found political allies for their positions, and their conflicts prolong and complicate the efforts to render labor legislation in final form. Moreover, some independents do not consider the FNPR a legitimate union (a view shared by many other Russians involved in politics as well as representatives of American unions), and they have periodically encouraged the Yeltsin administration to divest it of property and prerogatives accumulated during the Communist period. Russia faces the dilemma of trying to establish firm trade union rights while the largest potential beneficiary of those rights is a holdover from Soviet times viewed by many as an obstacle to genuine trade unionism.

Despite these qualifications, Russia is making progress toward the establishment of Western-style labor laws. The old system of state control over trade unions and official repression of independent activists is largely gone. A report in early 1994 of the arrest and attempted deportation of the independent trade union leader Vladimir Klebanov, on charges of visa violations, stands as an isolated incident echoing from the past; it was openly protested to the minister of internal affairs by several trade unions.[3] On the other hand, unions' rights to form and represent their members are by no means firmly settled.

Rights to Organize and Operate

The right to establish trade unions was spelled out in the December 1991 Supreme Soviet decree "On Registration of Public Associations in the RSFSR." Its provisions are simple and involve little formal procedure: those wishing to form a union must hold a conference or congress of unspecified size, approve statutory documents, and send them along with other information, including on bank accounts and composition of membership, to the Ministry of Justice or corresponding local organization within a month.[4] The union has rights as a legal entity from the moment the founding congress approves its statutory documents. An October 1991 presidential decree specifically guaranteed the strict observance of trade unions' rights during the transition to a market economy. The 1992 revised labor code reaffirmed these guarantees, required enterprises to facilitate unions' activities, and protected those elected to trade union organs from retaliation (transfer, dismissal, or disciplinary proceedings) by management.[5] The right of workers to unite in trade unions to defend their interests is enshrined in the December 1993 Russian Federation Constitution. A law further spelling out these rights, "On Trade Unions, Their Rights, and Guarantees of Their Activities," was passed by the Duma in December 1995 and is now in effect.[6]

In practice, however, those seeking to establish new trade unions have commonly met with managerial obstructionism and harassment, sometimes abetted by FNPR officials and local government administrators. According to the International Confederation of Free Trade Unions' 1994 *Annual Survey of Violations of Trade Union Rights*, in Russia, "at enterprise level . . . there is a tendency among managers and former official trade unionists to preserve the status quo, so very little space exists for the practice of genuine freedom of association. Independent union organizers were generally sacked before they got further than the organization of one shop per enterprise. Independent unions were also subject to harassment from local government officials. A range of low-level administrative obstacles were used against them . . . as well as more serious intimidatory tactics."[7] This characterization is confirmed by many reports of the experiences of individual activists, both those seeking to create new, enterprise-based unions and those associated with established independents. Union activists interviewed in Moscow in 1993 claimed that they feared discrimination in job assignments from enterprise managers and that FNPR officials threatened to exclude their children from summer camps run by the unions.[8] A recent study of Sotsprof found that cases of illegal dismissal of organizers were common and sometimes led to the collapse of union-building efforts; for example, Yevgenii Kirin was actively recruiting members from Moscow bus and trolleybus depots into a Sotsprof union he chaired when he was fired on the pretext of drunkenness at work and the union collapsed.[9]

When new unions do take root their leaders are often transferred, dismissed, or denied benefits and bonuses, in direct violation of the 1992 labor code. In a typical example, at the TsetMet Plant management dismissed the chair of the factory-based trade union and, when he protested the illegality of the firing, simply refused to recognize the union that had elected him. The chairman of the plant's FNPR union signed off on the firing, claiming that he had no say in the dismissal of someone who was not a member of his union.[10] Rank-and-file members of new unions are even more vulnerable because they generally lack rights of legal appeal, and the ongoing restructuring and layoffs at many enterprises provide a ready cover for retaliation against them. Activists in FPAD, for example, have been victimized by demotion, loss of bonuses, and transfers, while at Moscow's Vnukovo airport seven flight attendants associated with the independent union, including a member of its executive committee, were singled out for dismissal during restructuring. Management sometimes carries out a war of attrition against new unions, as in the case of a Moscow ambulance drivers' union whose members were subject to spot fines and loss of various privileges until their leader resigned.[11]

There have also been reports of threats, violence, and attempted murders of union activists, particularly those who tried to intervene in the privatization process. While the FNPR has often been complicit in repression of new unions, it has alleged attempts by managers to break up its own unions in connection with privatization.[12] The prospects for respect of unions' rights are bleaker still in the rapidly developing private sector, which is almost entirely unorganized. Workers there are generally better paid than those in the public sector or in formerly state-controlled industries, but conditions are often worse as pressures for profitability are higher. In sum, violations of unions' organizing rights in Russia are rampant, though, as shall be seen, the court system does provide some legal recourse for those subject to abuses.

COLLECTIVE BARGAINING RIGHTS

The March 1992 Russian Federation law "On Collective Contracts and Agreements" laid the legal foundations for concluding collective labor contracts at enterprises and other employing organizations.[13] According to the law, trade unions or "other representative organs empowered by the workers" have the right to initiate contract talks, and employers or managers are obliged to participate. Disagreements are settled by a reconciliation commission or, failing that, a mediator selected by mutual agreement. Limited time frames are specified for both negotiations and mediation. Workers may strike if mediation fails (though there are significant restrictions on the right to strike, which will be detailed further on). The contract may cover the usual issues—wages, benefits, conditions of employment and dismissal, working conditions and safety—as well as adjustment of wages to inflation and protection of workers' interests in the case of privatization of the enterprise and enterprise-owned housing. The contract must be in accordance with existing labor legislation and may be revised or renegotiated if the firm changes ownership or is reorganized, a likely prospect for many Russian companies. The law includes sanctions in the form of fines for employers who refuse to comply with its terms in hammering out contracts or who violate a signed contract, though these are not high enough to be effective, especially in an inflationary economy. The Ministry of Labor and Employment has the task of monitoring compliance, though a Labor Inspectorate capable of doing so was set up only in 1994.

The trade unions themselves have been at odds over a central provision of this legislation—the assignment of rights to represent workers in contract talks. The FNPR insists that only the largest trade union at an enterprise (in almost all cases itself) should have the right to negotiate, arguing that extension of this right to additional unions would encourage competition among unions in the contract process. The independents maintain that each union functioning at an enterprise should conclude its own agreement; this is the norm internationally.[14] The law itself incorporates an ambiguous and probably unworkable compromise, mandating that if several unions are present they should form a "combined representative organ" to negotiate and conclude a contract, while at the same time providing that a union has the right to hold talks independently and secure a separate contract for its members or a supplement to the general contract. The issue has become politicized, with the government alternately defending the independents' rights and siding with the FNPR. The Federation won the last round with a presidential decree requiring a single set of negotiations.[15]

The law on Collective Contracts and Agreements has made scarce headway in the years since its passage. Official sources tell the story. A 1993 report from the Labor Ministry found that approximately one-third of enterprises investigated had no collective contracts, while more than two-thirds of workers surveyed said that such agreements provided no (35 percent) or only partial (32 percent) guarantees of their interests.[16] Among new private businesses in Moscow, only 27 percent had collective agreements in place. Managers frequently failed to pay wages on schedule, sent workers on forced, unpaid leaves, and assigned reduced workdays, all in violation of labor contracts. In the fall of 1994 Vladimir Varov, head of the newly formed Federal Labor Inspectorate, decried the labor rights situation as "disastrous. Our employees have practically no legal protection in their relations with employers."[17] A report by the president's Human Rights Commission also found widespread violations of labor contracts and legislation in the areas of dismissals, social protections, and labor conditions. Occupational safety had deteriorated radically because of spending cuts and the elimination of health and safety departments within individual firms, and was virtually ignored at many private sector enterprises. Managers commonly refused to pay mandated compensation for job-related illnesses and injuries.[18] A 1995 OECD study concluded that in Russia, "collective bargaining at the firm level . . . appear[s] to be ineffective on the process of wage formation. It may only have some effect at successfully performing enterprises and fail to work at enterprises experiencing economic decline."[19]

There are a number of obstacles to the drawing up and implementation of collective contracts in Russian enterprises. First, unions often lack either the competence or the credibility to negotiate effectively. The resource-poor independents in many cases have too little financial and technical information or expertise to assess managements' claims. Thomas Bradley, past director of the U.S. program of assistance to independent Russian unions, told of receiving a phone call from potassium miners who were engaged in bargaining. They said to him, "[The managers] tell us the price of potassium is going down on the world market, and we have no way of knowing what's going on."[20] In any case managers often refuse to negotiate with independents, making contracts only with FNPR unions. The FNPR, which has the technical competence to negotiate, lacks credibility with its rank and file and is often unwilling to press management. Many enterprises in the final analysis are in such poor financial condition that their managers cannot fulfill labor contracts even if the will to honor is present.[21]

For its part, the government has little authority or enforcement power in this area. Labor Minister Gennady Melikyan has called on it to audit and regulate the finances of enterprise directors who fail to pay wages, charging that many conceal ample funds and pay themselves exorbitant salaries. Yeltsin has called on the courts for stricter enforcement, particularly of workers' rights to receive wages at times specified in their contracts. But critics doubt the effectiveness of such measures, pointing to the high case loads in Russian courts and the overwhelming technical difficulties in monitoring the more than 24,000 enterprises with wage arrears.[22] Moreover, government monitoring and supervisory personnel are regularly denied access to the premises and records of companies, especially those in the private sector, which evade taxes as well as regulation. The strong presence of organized crime further complicates government intervention. Finally, the government itself habitually delays payment of wages to public sector workers (such as teachers and doctors) and otherwise reneges on its obligations to workers.

THE RIGHT TO STRIKE

The May 1991 law "On the Procedure for Settlement of Collective Labor Disputes [or Conflicts]," which remained in force for most of the period under review, both recognized and limited the right to strike. The law specified the legitimate grounds for labor disputes, required management to negotiate with unions, and mandated that both conciliation and arbitration procedures must precede a strike. It called for a rather high threshold of approval, requiring that two-thirds of a union's members must endorse the strike decision by secret ballot. Strikes were illegal if they were held to press political demands, clearly a reaction to the large number of political strikes against the tottering government in 1990–91. They were also prohibited for railways, urban public transportation systems, civil aviation, communications, power, defense, or if they created a threat to the life and health of the population.[23] A trade union must compensate from its assets for damages caused by an illegal strike, and the strike's organizers may be dismissed and fined. Persons who forced others to strike through use or threat of force may be imprisoned. Another law, passed in the fall of 1995, made some significant revisions.[24] The new law lowered the requirement for approval of a strike declaration to one-half of those present at an assembly of the striking organization and eliminated the blanket prohibitions against strikes in transport, aviation, communications, and power, as well as those against political strikes. It left in place vaguer proscriptions against strikes that create threats to the constitutional order or the lives, health, and safety of the people.[25]

As in other areas, the Russian Federation government has created a new institution to help implement the legislation, in this case a Federal Service for Resolving Collective Labor Disputes, which is authorized to act as an intermediary in settlements and to help organize arbitration. Conciliation and arbitration mechanisms have been used to settle large numbers of labor conflicts, whereas only about 8 percent of registered conflicts result in strikes.[26] The most serious problem is the failure of managers and government (as employer) to fulfill the agreements they reached with labor, whether made to avert or to settle strikes. This failure has led to repeated, even chronic, strikes and strike threats over the same issues in some sectors. The weak bargaining position of many workers— the simple fact that much labor has become superfluous in the current economy—exacerbates the situation. Workers also frequently have failed to comply with the legislation by striking without the mandated arbitration or (before the 1995 legislation) by making sporadic political demands. Strikers also often call on the government directly to resolve labor disputes, partly because they lack faith in legislated procedures and courts, partly because the government, as owner (still) or subsidizer of numerous businesses, disposes of the relevant resources.

The 1991 prohibitions on the right to strike, while not out of line with American practice, were considered restrictive by the International Confederation of Free Trade Unions.[27] More significant, the prohibition against strikes in transport and civil aviation brought the government into conflict with some of the most militant independent unions. A large-scale strike of the Federation of Air Traffic Controllers' Unions in August 1992 was declared illegal, with the government pursuing criminal proceedings against strike leaders and threatening to dissolve the union.

Some participants were punished by removal from housing lists, denial of access to day care, or cancellation of bonuses.[28] More recent strikes by air traffic controllers, pilots, and railroad workers have also been found illegal in the courts. While legal proceedings in these cases have seldom been carried to their conclusion, they seem intended to intimidate the independent union movement.[29] The vaguer prohibitions in the new legislation remain largely untested.

CREATING A FAVORABLE CLIMATE FOR COMPLIANCE

Russia's record so far in creating a Western system of labor relations is ambiguous. Many of the necessary laws and institutions are now in place. The new Civil Code has been adopted, and a new Law on Trade Unions is in effect. A federal labor inspectorate and labor dispute resolutions board have been established. Routine compliance and enforcement—establishment of the "rule of law" in labor relations—will be far more complicated. As shown before, managers and others often take a contemptuous or dismissive attitude toward workers' and unions' rights. Those affected by violations seldom seek legal recourse; in a recent survey, only one in five trade union leaders said he or she would defend collective bargaining rights in court.[30] But there are some promising developments and measures that can be taken to promote the rule of law.

Despite the overall weaknesses of the legal system, Russian courts often do provide redress to those whose rights are violated. The courts are far from perfect in either substance or procedure, but cumulative statistical and case evidence show that unions and workers who pursue their grievances through the court system frequently win. In 1993, for example, courts considered nearly 16,000 cases in which workers charged unjustified denial of compensation for job-related illnesses and injuries and awarded compensation in 91 percent of these.[31] The independent unions, most prominently Sotsprof, have brought scores of cases over unfair dismissals, refusal of management to bargain with the union, and other compliance issues and often have gained enforcement of the laws. A 1994 study by the U.S. State Department concluded that independent trade union officials were pursuing their cases in Russian courts with increasing success rates.[32] The "Rule of Law" component of the AFL-CIO's program of assistance to Russian trade unions also provides evidence that, when union activists and workers know their rights and have access to competent legal advice, they can use the courts to make powerful managers or directors comply with the law.

Progress toward routine enforcement of labor's rights will require education, institution building, and, at least in the short term, expanded access to legal resources. First, activists and workers must learn what protections are afforded them by new legislation; this will require a sustained educational effort on the part of unions and those who seek to aid them. Second, labor and public interest law must be developed as part of the legal profession's training, to overcome the severe shortage of lawyers who can provide advice and defense to workers and unions, as well as to remedy the poor competence of judges handling their cases. Strengthening the state's regulatory capacities is also necessary. Third, labor interests must have access to legal resources on an affordable basis in order to bring large numbers of cases to court for an initial period, creating a demonstration effect. If managers and others come to expect that violations of labor rights will regularly be contested and that the courts will enforce the law, compliance will improve and the need to rely on the court system should diminish. The rule of law, in other words, will become customary by practice and case-by-case enforcement.

STRIKE ACTIVITY AND ITS EFFECTS

One of the major instruments of pressure available to workers is to withhold labor through organized strikes. In Western systems of labor relations strikes are normally legal only when collective bargaining has failed to produce a contract with management and are normally ended by binding arbitration or concessions. The new Russian legislation summarized above sets similar conditions. However, most strikes that have taken place in Russia do not fit this pattern; rather, they are prompted by violations of existing contracts and other grievances, are frequently directed at government or demand government mediation, and result in agreements that often fail to bind. Moreover, inflation and other economic conditions have rapidly undermined the gains of much labor activism.

THE BEGINNINGS OF LABOR ACTIVISM

The first major outburst of working-class activism came with the massive summer 1989 Soviet miners' strike.[33] Some half-million miners in the country's several major coal basins, which were spread throughout the republics of Russia, Ukraine, and Kazakhstan, ceased work nearly simultaneously and presented a list of demands to the Kremlin. Though the right to strike had not yet been formally established, the miners felt confident that their grievances would be heard. They knew that smaller strikes in mining and other sectors had brought negotiations rather than the old-style repression. Glasnost had allowed journalists to write exposés about the terrible conditions in mining regions, bringing national attention to the ecological devastation, high accident rates, and often primitive living conditions. The Gorbachev regime had recently made good on its promise of democratization by holding the first competitive elections in Soviet history to form a Congress of People's Deputies. Deputies recently elected from mining districts would be sitting in Moscow to hear workers' grievances. There was a tremendous sense of optimism and empowerment among the miners.

The most impressive feature of the strikes was their level of organization. Previously workers had been tightly controlled, with any independent organizing initiatives squelched and their leaders arrested. Analysts expected that it would take considerable time to overcome the effects of decades of enforced passivity, that Soviet workers would have little capacity to lead or coordinate collective actions in the newly democratizing state. The miners belied these expectations, spawning grassroots strike committees that maintained order, worked out unified demands, and bargained authoritatively on behalf of the strikers. The modus operandi and grievances of the various miners' groups were very similar and must have been communicated from one coal basin to another across vast expanses of territory. The breadth of the strike still defies explanation. The mood of solidarity, though common among miners in the West who have a long history of organization and struggle, was remarkable in the Soviet context.

The other aspect of the strike that surprised many observers was the miners' support for market reform. Many specialists viewed Soviet workers as psychologically and otherwise dependent on the Brezhnev-era welfare state and expected them to resist reforms that threatened their economic security. Although the miners did oppose some aspects of reform (in particular, higher prices in the private retail sector), they favored, indeed demanded, limits to state control over mines as well as the right to organize production and dispose of at least part of their product independently. The miners believed that, given more autonomy, they could sell their coal domestically for much higher prices than those allowed by the state. More important, they wanted to end the government's monopoly on marketing coal abroad for hard currency and to bring the benefits of hard currency sales directly back to the basins. With these resources, the miners argued, they could end their dependence on state subsidies, could themselves afford the technological upgrading of equipment that the government had long ignored, and could provide social amenities that the state was unable to afford. They could become economically self-sufficient and contribute much to improving their own lives.

The miners' strike exposed a great deal of information about the living conditions of Russian workers in the Siberian and Arctic regions, which had been closed to Westerners. Many miners lived in extremely dilapidated housing, including pre-World War II barracks and buildings used for convict labor in the 1930s. Places in schools were too few, and children were split into morning and afternoon sessions, with no hope of improvement. Water and electricity were often supplied during restricted hours and were completely lacking in some households, and sewage was inadequate. Severe pollution in the basins caused major heath problems, especially for children, who frequently suffered from chronic ailments without appropriate health care. Supplies of consumer goods were always poor, and there were even fewer to be had during the years of Gorbachev's attempted reforms. The humiliating soap shortage, which made it impossible for miners even to wash after days of hard and dirty work in the pits, stands as a symbol of their grievances. The incidence of serious and fatal accidents in Soviet mines far exceeded Western levels, a fact that could be covered up by information controls in the period prior to glasnost but was now well known to miners. The list of accumulated grievances was long, and, finally given a voice, miners demanded that all be redressed.

The Gorbachev regime confronted the strike in the absence of relevant laws, mediating mechanisms, or arbitration boards; the Communists had never before negotiated openly with workers. The striking miners rejected the official trade unions, treating their functionaries with contempt and allowing them little role except to serve sandwiches on picket lines. The miners claimed that the official unions had failed to defend their interests, as evidenced by the wretched conditions of their lives and work, and that they had long been a pawn of both management and the Communist Party. The strikers also bypassed their managers and local authorities, directing their grievances to the reformist central government and demanding that ministerial-level officials come and negotiate with them. Gorbachev acceded to most of their demands, sending both Prime Minister Nikolai Ryzhkov and Coal Minister Mikhail Shchadov to meet with miners' representatives and endorsing a long list of concessions. In the end, miners were promised more economic autonomy as producers, including the right to charge higher prices, increased wages and benefits, and improved social conditions.

The miners' strike was both the triumphant beginning of the Soviet/Russian workers' movement and its high point. The Independent Miners' Union (NPG), one of the most important of the independents, grew out of the strike committees formed in the summer of 1989. But this union still organizes only a small minority of all miners; the majority remain in the FNPR. The official Federation was shocked into realization of its weakness by the miners' strike and began to take more independent positions to distinguish itself from the declining Communist Party, measures that contributed to its survival. The government under Gorbachev overcommitted itself seriously in the strike settlement and proved unable or unwilling to deliver many of the promised changes and benefits. In the aftermath of the mass strike smaller groups of miners struck again and again to press for implementation of the settlement, especially the promises of greater economic autonomy. Economic losses from this "war of attrition" were substantial. The miners' frustration led to the growing politicization of their movement and, in 1991, to demands for Gorbachev's resignation that helped to bring down the regime. At this point Russian miners turned to Boris Yeltsin, who promised them greater autonomy in an independent Russia.

But the miners' problems were not over. Their assumptions about the prospects for economic self-sufficiency proved flawed. Many mines were in fact obsolete and exhausted, unable to survive without large government subsidies. Coal prices were increased, but many domestic consumers simply could not pay the higher prices and their debts accumulated. The prospects for foreign currency earnings, while realistic for some mines, ran up against problems with poor coal quality, old equipment, and high transport costs. Miners have remained one of the most organized and restive groups among Russian workers, but they never regained the optimism and unity of 1989. The diminishing expectations that are reflected in their chronic strike movements tell much of the story of Russian industrial labor in the period since economic reforms were first tried.

In the two years after the mass miners' strike labor activism did develop among other workers, and additional independent unions emerged. Oil and gas workers, representing another strategic and potentially profitable energy sector, struck with a set of demands similar to those of the miners: they wanted prices for their output raised to world levels and expanded foreign marketing rights. Gold miners and metallurgical workers struck with more traditional demands for higher wages, while doctors and teachers demanded wage increases as well as greater state allocations for medical facilities and schools. In the transport sector strikes went hand in hand with the formation of new independent unions among pilots, air traffic controllers, and railroad workers, and gains from initial strikes helped to solidify and legitimate these unions. Local organizing initiatives proliferated as Communist Party cells were evicted from factories by Yeltsin, the newly elected president of Russia, and the old state controls weakened and collapsed.

LABOR ACTIVISM IN YELTSIN'S RUSSIA: LOSING GROUND

With the government's implementation of shock-therapy reform in January 1992, Russian labor activism and strike activity took on an increasingly defensive character. That is to say, the goal of most strikes became to limit losses rather than to win new benefits. As discussed in Chapter 1, the January price liberalization combined with inflation to drive down real wages and living standards. Workers struck to keep from falling further behind, and, in a vicious cycle, the wage concessions they gained fueled further inflation that undercut those gains. Wage increases of even 100 percent and more proved ephemeral; as one spokesman for the miners stated, "All these high prices have nullified everything miners achieved during the three years of strike struggle."[34] In such an environment it became difficult for workers to sustain the motivation for collective action, or confidence in the unions that could organize it. The level of strike activity remained extremely low in view of the high costs reform was imposing on labor. In 1992, for example, only 27 strike days were lost per 1000 workers, compared with an OECD average of 110 in that year. In the following years the incidence of strikes in Russia fell, to only 4 days lost per 1000 workers in 1993 and less than 1 day in the first quarter of 1994.[35]

Table 2.1 shows the very modest level of strike activity over recent years, along with an upsurge of strike activity in 1995 and early 1996. Strikes have been spread across many sectors but concentrated in a few, especially mining, education and health care, transport, and defense. Teachers and health care workers, for instance, mounted a broad strike movement in the winter and spring of 1992, struck sporadically in the following years, and went on a prolonged strike in early 1995 that accounts for much of the overall increase in strike activity for that year.[36] Among the most poorly paid of all Russian workers to begin with, many in these largely female professions found themselves below the official poverty line as prices increased. The conditions of their work environment were also deteriorating as government allocations for social services declined. Disrupted trade links deprived doctors of much-needed

TABLE 2.1
LABOR STRIKES IN THE RUSSIAN FEDERATION, 1993–95

	Number of Strikes	Average Loss of Work Time per Strike (in days)	Average Number of Participants per Strike
1993	265	112	n.a.
1994	514	184	305
1995Q1	519	1,288	315
1995Q2	347	527	73
1995Q3	5,021	43	37
1995Q4	3,080	98	45
1996Q1	3,722	221	65
1996Q2	208	919	130

Source: Russian Economic Trends 4, no. 4 (London: Whurr Publishers: 1995): 95; ibid. 5, no. 2 (1996): 110.

equipment and pharmaceuticals that had long been imported from Czechoslovakia and the GDR. In January 1992 the government preempted a Russia-wide strike threat over "poverty" wages by granting doctors a 45 percent across-the-board salary increase, but much of it was rapidly lost to inflation. In the spring desperate teachers closed schools and day care centers, while health workers withheld nonemergency services and threatened to stop all types of medical assistance. The strike was supported, though not really led, by the FNPR and apparently endorsed by many school and medical administrators. The government responded with more wage increases and other concessions, but these provided only temporary relief. Some participated in more limited strikes later on, and some groups of teachers, pharmacists, and others affiliated with Sotsprof, but no major, new organizing initiatives emerged in these sectors. Instead, many left their jobs, and sometimes their professions, to move into the private sector or took on additional work of any kind in a labor market no longer controlled by the state. The steady worsening of conditions led to a new wave of nationwide unrest in early 1995, and again in 1996, over low wages, extensive wage arrears, and drastically inadequate government allocations for social services.[37]

The government has confronted strikes lately in a number of other sectors, especially those with independent unions. Though these unions had all taken strongly proreform positions, they faced an obvious organizational imperative to try to maintain their members' living standards through collective action. Miners have struck repeatedly, demanding that their wages be increased to cover cumulative price increases and that their future earnings and pensions be indexed to inflation. Yeltsin tried to buy off the militants by conceding a tripling of miners' already high (in the Russian context) wages. Oil and gas workers also won a tripling of their paychecks as well as domestic price increases for their output. Numerous strike threats by pilots and air traffic controllers, both led by independent unions, have been headed off by wage increases. Municipal transportation workers have struck in various cities and threatened an all-Federation transport strike. Virtually all strikes have been met with substantial concessions. The government, being particularly vulnerable to broad strike threats that could close down schools, hospitals, or bus and train services in many Russian cities simultaneously, or to energy sector shutdowns that cripple parts of domestic industry, usually responded with easy terms that preempted or brought a rapid end to strikes. Then, faced with the contradictory goals of controlling inflation and paying large wage increases, the government simply ceased or delayed wage payments. The nonpayments (or arrears) crisis spread throughout much of the economy, with fully employed workers receiving no wages at all for two and three months at a time, uncertain as to when or how much they might be paid. Researchers in Moscow became accustomed to checking with their institutes daily to see if any moneys had been received, and if so, how partial payments would be divided among employees.[38]

The wage arrears crisis further demoralized the workers' movement. It showed that, even where unions could organize and carry out ostensibly successful strikes, they often could not compel compliance with the agreements reached. The laws, norms, and stability required for functional labor relations were lacking; an inflationary economy and an unreliable government undermined unions' efforts and left many workers feeling powerless. The FNPR threatened a broad, even national, strike against wage arrears, but it lacked the authority and probably the will to lead one. Instead, it helped mount waves of collective protests and brief warning strikes across various sectors—including medical, education, agroindustrial, defense, communications, and energy workers—and regions. Though the workers' protests were strident, actual strikes rarely lasted longer than a day or two. The government repeatedly promised to pay, but it would do so only partially and sporadically, leading to renewed protests from frustrated and increasingly desperate workers. One of Yeltsin's major campaign promises in the 1996 presidential election was to eliminate wage arrears, but in the election's aftermath the problem remains acute.

Strikes and Protests in the Postprivatization Economy

By 1994 a substantial part of the Russian economy had been privatized. Inflation had declined to more manageable levels, and Western-style labor legislation had been put into place. Have these changes led to more settled patterns of labor activism and dispute resolution? A survey of some recent strike activity will show that the answer is largely negative. Most strikes still do not resemble the Western pattern of labor-management disputes that can be resolved by contract negotiations or binding arbitration. Instead, strikers (often with the support of managers) continue to direct many of their demands to government, for several reasons. Though it has taken dramatic measures to diminish its overwhelming presence in the economy, the state continues to play a large role in many sectors as owner, subsidizer, or chief contractor for products. Furthermore, the old habit of holding the government responsible sticks. Most important, government-sponsored reform policies are often seen by workers as the main source of their problems and grievances, and the dislocations in many sectors are so deep that they can be addressed only at the governmental level. The following review of strike movements in a few of the most activist sectors will give a sense of the range of grievances and depth of crisis in parts of Russia's economy.

Workers in both the print and broadcast media held highly visible job actions during 1994. The press, including most major Moscow newspapers and journals, threatened to strike during the first meetings of the newly elected parliament in January.[39] Most of the publications themselves were privately owned. The enterprises that printed them, however, had been privatized only recently under a government decree that raised the value of their assets and led to a large increase (200–400 percent) in the price of printing services. Journalists claimed that a price hike of this magnitude would force them to suspend publication, and journalists' unions joined with editors in chief to set up a strike committee. They demanded that the government, as sponsor of the privatization legislation, either provide targeted subsidies to compensate for the higher costs or alter the procedure for privatization in printing and related fields. They charged that the increases represented a threat to freedom of speech and constituted "the latest effort to strangle Russia's emerging independent media"[40] (while apparently failing to see direct government subsidies as a threat to freedom and independence). Of major papers only *Rossiyskaya Gazeta* refused to participate, arguing that the dispute should be between the print trades and the journals exclusively. The issue was settled in meetings between the chief editors of major publications and government officials, including Prime Minister Viktor Chernomyrdin.

In February much of Russia was hit by blackouts of central radio and television programming.[41] The issue was all too familiar: the state television company Ostankino owed some 80 billion rubles to telecommunications workers and transmitting facilities throughout Russia. The communication workers' trade union called the strike only after repeated governmental instructions to resolve the crisis had gone unfulfilled. Union leaders demanded and got negotiations with Chernomyrdin and other officials, who agreed to a repayment of the debts in stages. But by August television and radio workers were again threatening to strike as regional facilities faced bankruptcy because of continued nonpayment.

There has also been considerable tension and unrest in the massive Russian defense sector. Under the old Soviet system many defense plants were located in closed cities where security was tight but workers enjoyed highly privileged living conditions and supplies of consumer goods. Over the past few years it has confronted dramatic declines in government expenditure on weapons procurement and development. Plans to convert a large part of industrial capacity to civilian production have proved more expensive and technologically difficult than anticipated, yielding uneven success. The industry is plagued by billions of rubles in wage arrears and deferred payments for output already delivered; in the city of Kovrov alone, for example, the state owes more than 50 billion rubles to several major defense plants, and tens of thousands of workers have been sent on compulsory leave at minimal pay, while there are virtually no new orders and mountains of weapons sit in warehouses. In the spring of 1994 the FNPR-affiliated Trade Union of Defense Industry Workers demanded that the Duma maintain current levels of defense spending in the 1995 draft budget, open more credit lines for conversion programs, and organize sales of armaments abroad. Otherwise, the union argued, 80 percent of defense enterprises would face bankruptcy, nearly a million and a half workers would be laid off, and unemployment benefits would amount to 30 trillion rubles.[42] Though these claims proved exaggerated, the crisis of the defense sector is very real. Following the usual strategy, the union's leadership talked about calling an all-Russia strike, but local unions throughout the industry would back only a five- to ten-minute work stoppage to dramatize their demands. Sporadic strikes continue, but, even if they had more confidence in the union, workers must fear that a prolonged strike could precipitate the collapse of already weak enterprises.[43]

Strikes and strike threats have also remained chronic in coal mining districts, with FNPR unions recently playing more of a leadership role, while the NPG sometimes opposes the strikes.[44] The miners' demands now focus on several issues. Although part of the industry has been privatized and converted to joint-stock companies, it remains heavily dependent on state subsidies, which, like wages and other payments, are often in arrears. Liberalization of energy prices should have benefited the miners except that many industrial enterprises and municipalities— the ultimate consumers of energy from coal—simply cannot afford the increases. In Irkutsk, miners warned of a strike because heating and electric power stations had fallen far behind in their payments for coal; in turn, industrial enterprises were not paying the power stations.[45] The miners threatened to stop shipping coal and close down the city's enterprises, but this would have left them without customers. Instead, in a response typical even within privatized industries, they called on the Russian Federation government to help resolve the problem and avert the strike.

But the militant miners are in a weak position economically. When miners in Tula went on strike against the administration of the Tulaugol joint-stock company over missing wages, a result of unpaid state subsidies and delinquent bills by coal recipients, the proreform paper *Izvestiya* was unsympathetic. It pointed out that some of the mines had long operated at a loss and well below capacity, and that the miners had already received their legitimate presubsidy earnings. The paper warned, "With today's slump in production the government will get along fine without [their] coal. The strike actually helps: the government will save tens of billions of rubles in subsidies, and the only ones to suffer will be the miners."[46] Indeed, *Izvestiya* continued, it would be preferable to close these mines, but the cost, including promised government resettlement aid for displaced workers, would be prohibitive.

Other strikes demonstrate even more desperation. The problem of long-term nonpayment of wages remains central for Russia's workers, and it has led to numerous reported instances of hunger strikes supported by trade unions after other measures failed, even to suicides. Timber, atomic energy, Pacific Fleet, and Komi region oil workers as well as doctors have all threatened and pleaded for payment of back wages. One observer of the Russian labor scene concluded, ". . . even paying out a part of the back-pay extinguishes the strongest of protests."[47] Unpaid workers in remote districts, especially in the Far North, plead for resettlement aid so that they can seek work opportunities elsewhere. Many strikes have also taken on political overtones. At a strike over back pay by several hundred mining construction workers in the Arctic city of Vorkuta, a representative of the usually progovernment Independent Miners' Union said that the strikers "did not care who the President or the Prime Minister is when their families are starving"[48] and that some would seek redress from the right-wing candidate Vladimir Zhirinovsky if the government remained indifferent. During a February 1996 strike, Vorkuta miners adopted a resolution calling for the resignation of Yeltsin and the government. According to the resolution, "the reforms that are being implemented are plunging our country ever deeper into the quagmire of economic crisis, while driving the coal industry toward complete disintegration. Even now the state has no properly thought-out program for development of the coal industry or its restructuring."[49] In December a nationwide miners' strike, lasting more than a week, again called for the government's resignation.[50]

CONCLUSION

It should be obvious that the labor legislation reviewed earlier in this chapter has not and cannot be effective in resolving these disputes. Management is not the target of many labor grievances and does not dispose of the resources to resolve them. Often, as with subsidies, budget allocations, and resettlement aid, government is the direct target, and workers' demands are a legacy of decades of state control that have left their enterprises—overbuilt defense plants, obsolete coal mines, remote construction projects in the Far North—backward or bankrupt in the face of the market. Even in the privatized economy workers and managers often look to the government to influence prices, provide credit, or enforce payment on buyers of their products, functions that would normally be performed by financial institutions, contracts, and courts in the West. The incompleteness of the institutional system and the chaos caused by widespread nonpayments help push these functions onto government. Finally, strikes have commonly been used to bring issues to the bargaining table after repeated violations of contracts and agreements rather than as a last resort when collective bargaining fails. There is, here again, little evidence of the rule- and contract-governed system of labor relations patterned on Western practice and envisioned in recent labor legislation.

The preceding review of strike activity should also yield insights into the problems of Russian trade union development. As seen, the level of strikes over the past few years has been remarkably low, and those that have taken place reflect the diminishing expectations and growing hardships of many workers. Over time strikes have become smaller (see Table 2.1) and more defensive. The trade unions that organize or coordinate these strikes, whether FNPR or independent, have generally delivered limited benefits at best to their members. Overall, the meager demonstrable gains from collective action have contributed little to union building. There have been exceptions. Oil workers attained extremely high wages—four times the average industrial salary—through repeated strikes, and Sotsprof has claimed successes in strikes against managers over unpaid wages. The most successful independents, the Pilots', Air Traffic Controllers' and Independent Miners' unions, have gained more than others through frequent strike activity. It remains possible that the newfound militance of the FNPR in some sectors, in the face of endless wage arrears and crisis conditions, will produce larger and more effective industrial actions in the future.

CHAPTER 3

UNIONS' INFLUENCE IN GOVERNMENTAL AND ELECTORAL POLITICS

TRIPARTISM

As he set about establishing an independent Russian government in the fall of 1991, Boris Yeltsin called for a "social partnership" with labor. His motives were several. Foremost, he wanted to create the broadest possible consensus around reform policies—and consensus did still seemed possible in this, the "honeymoon" period of his presidency. Reform would inevitably impose big costs on labor, and Yeltsin hoped that workers would accept these costs more readily if their representatives played a direct role in national policymaking. Yeltsin's government also needed a ready institutional mechanism to mediate employment disputes and settle strikes. Labor unrest had played a significant role in the recent collapse of the Gorbachev regime, and reform seemed likely to provoke new conflicts. As Aleksandr Shokhin, then labor minister and the architect of tripartism, put it, "We need a social partnership at least so that the interaction between the trade unions and the government does not get determined by street battles. Today . . . the trade unions are making demands, calling . . . meetings or declaring strikes—and the government is making concessions. We would like to work out compromises together for implementing economic reforms . . . not repudiating reform, but taking into consideration . . . the interests of the various strata."[1] The trade unions, for their part, responded positively. The independents supported Yeltsin and reform in any case. The FNPR, at this point still relieved to have escaped the fate of the banned Communist Party, offered its cooperation and soon began pressing for the exclusive right to represent labor.

In January 1992 the partnership was institutionalized in the Tripartite Commission for the Regulation of Social and Labor Relations, a three-sided bargaining structure that included representatives of labor, government, and management.[2] It was modeled on the corporatist bargaining structures that have successfully moderated labor conflict in a number of West European countries and have strong ILO (International Labor Organization) endorsement. After considerable conflict over who should sit in labor's fourteen seats, nine were allocated to the FNPR, three to Sotsprof, and one each to the Independent Miners' Union (NPG) and the Independent Union of Civil Aviation Pilots. Representatives of organizations from state industry, including Arkady Volsky's then influential Russian Union of Industrialists and Entrepreneurs, and from newly emergent entrepreneurial groups sat in management's seats. The government side was in theory to mediate between labor and management on the commission; its seats were filled by ministers and deputy ministers. The commission's charge was to review wage levels, monitor working conditions, conclude an annual General Agreement on Social and Economic Policy, and resolve labor disputes and conflicts. Participating unions accepted a no-strike rule as long as standing agreements were being observed.

If Russian tripartism began amidst genuine hopes for compromise and conciliation, the harsh realities of reform soon brought conflict. The commission's early meetings coincided with the introduction of Yegor Gaidar's "shock therapy" reforms. The first of these, the January 1992 price liberalization, caused a precipitous drop in real wages. Austerity policies and the ongoing decline in industrial production threatened Russian workers' livelihoods, while a proposed privatization program brought further uncertainty. These issues dominated the commission's sessions, and the FNPR, despite its promise to support reform, was at odds with the government on all of them. FNPR representatives pressed for continuation of price controls, periodic upward adjustment of wages to compensate for price increases, and continued government subsidies and credits to halt the decline in production and keep enterprises afloat. They also resisted the government's program for rapid privatization of industry, which reformers saw as the key to making the transition to a market-driven economy. Governmental compromise on these issues could only drive up the budget deficit as well as inflation and delay necessary restructuring of Russia's economy.

The Tripartite Commission did conclude a General Agreement in March 1992.[3] While somewhat long on promises and short on specifics, the agreement included some significant concessions by the government on wages and price controls, and it promised unemployment insurance and other safety-net policies. It committed the union side to cooperate with reform and privatization, and to refrain from striking over any of the issues covered in the agreement. The influential deputy prime minister Gennady Burbulis, the commission's coordinator, welcomed the agreement as "a healthy, constructive foundation for the advance of reforms in Russia."[4] The commission also helped to ease labor unrest. In the spring delegates negotiated an end to another miners' strike in the Kuzbass coal basin and mediated one that loomed in the Tyumen oil fields, both major energy-producing regions. Yeltsin also turned to them for a working proposal to preempt the threatened Russia-wide strike by teachers and medical personnel. Tripartite Commission representatives succeeded in settling these strikes, however, mainly because they made large wage concessions rather than because they exercised any particular authority among workers.

Despite these qualified successes, overall the commission worked poorly. From the outset FNPR officials charged bad faith, claiming that the government bypassed them in preparing critical legislation. Commission meetings were marked by dissension and bickering not only between FNPR and government representatives but also among the unions, particularly FNPR and Sotsprof, which challenged one another's right to represent workers. Government officials were frequently absent. Several FNPR representatives delayed signing the General Agreement, insisting that new promises by Yeltsin's government to the IMF to cut the budget deficit contradicted its provisions. Within weeks of the signing FNPR president Igor Klochkov was railing against the government's failures to abide by the agreement, claiming that it held meetings of the commission "purely for the sake of form" and threatening to withdraw his representatives.[5] Growing arrears in wage payments to government workers further exacerbated tensions; the FNPR threatened to call a nationwide strike unless the government paid overdue wages throughout Russia.

By midyear, the tripartite process was breaking down. The FNPR shortly thereafter defected from the three-sided bargaining structure to join a manager-led coalition, the Civic Union,[6] which helped oust reformist acting prime minister Gaidar in December. In the last months of 1992 the Tripartite Commission effectively ceased functioning. After FNPR-sponsored protest meetings in October, a bilateral government-FNPR conciliation commission was formed instead. The year ended on a mixed note, with one FNPR official asserting that "everything, almost, previously agreed on with the government in substance has been in vain up to now,"[7] while Klochkov and the new labor minister, Gennady Melikyan, signed an agreement to continue seeking compromise on the familiar list of divisive economic issues.

Tripartite bargaining did not bring compromise and stability to Russian labor relations, as it had done in the Western European context. This experience provides a cautionary tale for those who seek to transfer Western models to the very different conditions of post-Communist Russia. Tripartism quickly became mired in conflict because the three-sided bargaining structure proved a poor fit for Russia. The basic concept is that government will mediate between independent labor unions and organizations of private sector managers. In the Russian context, though, none of the three institutional partners could play its assigned role.

The government could not act as a genuine mediator because it had prime responsibility for the economy on two counts: the state still owned and controlled most of Russia's productive assets, and of course the government itself had designed and initiated the program for radical reform of the economy. Most managers worked for the state; in 1992 no major independent managerial and few entrepreneurial groups were available. Thus, unions' demands were targeted not toward managers but toward the government directly; as Shokhin acknowledged, trade unions "look to the state as employer."[8] Government was the chief bargaining partner for labor as well as the agent responsible for delivering on agreements. Indeed, labor and management often shared an interest in making claims on governmental resources, and they joined in the Tripartite Commission to press for subsidies, soft credits, and the like.[9] Nor could the unions play their usual role of unifying labor at the national level. Tripartism assumes the presence of broadly organized, acknowledgedly legitimate labor unions, and such were absent in Russia. Union representatives on the commission not only disagreed over issues but also regularly attacked each other; they lacked any potential for solidarity.

Instead of an effective mechanism for managing labor relations, then, Russia's Tripartite Commission served primarily as a forum for government-labor conflict, secondarily as a forum for conflict among the unions. It would have been difficult to achieve compromise over Russia's reform program even given the best of faith—too much was up for grabs, too many would end up big losers. In the event, the government, far more interested in extricating itself from control of economic activity than in managing labor relations, proved a disengaged bargaining partner. As a matter of fact, government representatives and even the coordinator often skipped meetings of the commission. And the bureaucracy regularly failed to deliver on officials' promises to the unions. The FNPR responded in kind to the government's bad faith, working to undermine reform even as it promised support and meeting broken agreements with its own, largely empty strike threats.

Meanwhile, independent unions outside the Tripartite process mounted successful strikes and gained large concessions from the government. All this was a far cry from European corporatism, in which managers and governments deliver promised benefits and unions return labor peace and stability.

The Tripartite Commission was nevertheless revived in 1993. Early in that year Yeltsin renewed the commission's powers, while the FNPR's Klochkov struck a conciliatory note, calling for "an effective system of partnership, getting away from the policy of opposing one another."[10] Why did both sides commit themselves once more to an apparently failed approach? Because tripartism served useful purposes for both the government and the FNPR. First, it allowed the government to share responsibility for painful reform policies; in the words of commission coordinator Burbulis, the three sides were "co-authors of the reforms."[11] Second, the formal appearance of partnership between government and the workforce placed Russian labor relations in the mold of the most liberal European polities, strengthening the system's uncertain claims to democracy. Third, though the FNPR had not to this point succeeded in mounting large protests or strikes, Yeltsin and the government were uncertain about the potential for unrest as workers felt the brunt of reform policies and thought it prudent to keep up negotiations with the only national organization available to represent them.

Though poorly treated in many respects, the FNPR also derived benefits from its participation in the commission. A very weak presence to many of its nominal members, it gained status as the officially sanctioned representative for most of Russia's labor force; in truth, the government was lending legitimacy to the FNPR simply by recognizing it as a national-level bargaining partner. Even if it lost on many issues, the Federation secured the possibility, through negotiation, of delivering to its members concrete goods (pay raises, unemployment benefits) that could help keep them on the rolls. The commission was one more forum in which the FNPR could defend its inherited advantages from challengers. Though the organization was often heard decrying its own weakness and humiliation in the tripartite process, without the commission it would have had even less influence. The independents as well gained visibility and legitimacy through their role and pressed for increased representation.

Developments in the Tripartite Commission during 1993 paralleled those of 1992. The FNPR gained an increased share of labor's representation, eleven of fourteen seats, purely on the basis of its size. Only three small independents got individual seats—a slap in the face to Sotsprof and other unions that had been loyal to Yeltsin and reform. A second General Agreement was concluded in the spring, covering employment policy, income and living standards, and measures for social protection. The document, several pages long, consisted mostly of statements of intent to "develop proposals" or "submit legislation to the Supreme Soviet" on one issue or another, but it made few definite commitments. The unions nevertheless appended a "Protocol of Disagreement," pressing for a higher minimum wage and a promise that the government would limit unemployment to the very low figure of 3.5 percent.[12] The failure of the parties to reach even a vague agreement on paper without dissent was indicative of things to come. Klochkov was soon charging that the government had raised prices and withheld wages in violation of its promises, and that it intended no serious negotiations or compromises. In the days before October's political crisis, he was threatening to call a national strike over the trillions of rubles in wage arrears.

As recounted earlier, 1993 ended with a confrontation between the FNPR and government in which the umbrella union lost badly. Events of that fall highlighted both the instability and politicization of Russian tripartism. Shortly after the FNPR had opposed Yeltsin's dissolution of parliament, First Deputy Prime Minister Vladimir Shumeiko, the Tripartite Commission's coordinator at the time, called a meeting. When FNPR representatives failed to attend, Shumeiko simply invited representatives of independent unions, which had responded more sympathetically to Yeltsin's dramatic move, to form a working group on expanding the commission. Faced with a crisis, in other words, the government decided that now it *would* reward political loyalty, regardless of agreements then in place. Labor's side of the commission was in fact reorganized in December, though the specifics remain vague.[13]

The Tripartite Commission continued to work in 1994, and a third General Agreement was concluded, but it was soon overshadowed by a Social Accord Pact signed by both government and unions, along with representatives of most other official bodies and social organizations, in late April.[14] The Social Accord Pact was an attempt at national reconciliation following the October crisis and the divisive December 1993 elections; all signatories committed themselves to maintaining political stability and respecting the constitution. The pact also acknowledged Russia's socioeconomic crisis and, once again, promised relief in broad strokes. Unions that signed took a qualified no-strike pledge, promising not to strike over budgetary policy, though they could put down tools over directly job-related issues such as wages or working conditions.

For the purposes of this study, the Social Accord Pact is significant because it pointed up the growing disunity within the FNPR. While the FNPR leadership signed on, several of its sectoral and regional affiliates either refused or subsequently withdrew. The massive agro-industrial unions joined with the Agrarian Party, their electoral ally, in rejecting the pact. The Mass Media Creative Workers' Trade Union refused to sign. Unions in Vladivostok threatened to withdraw their signature and call for the resignation of president and government. The FNPR, now under the chairmanship of Mikhail Shmakov, proved unable to pull together even for this largely symbolic gesture. By fall, predictably, the FNPR's leadership was reconsidering its own signature and threatening protests. This time government representatives responded that the union should turn to the managers of now privatized enterprises with their grievances.

To be sure, in the years since the Tripartite Commission was established, the structure of ownership and control in Russia's economy had changed radically. Privatization had transformed the majority of enterprises into joint-stock companies owned mainly by their managers and workers. (Privatization will be covered in greater detail in Chapter 4.) Most former state retail stores and consumer services were in private hands, and new private enterprise was developing in all sectors of the economy. The government no longer controlled most economic activity. Managers were on their own, and their decisions and behavior were, at least in theory, market driven.

The significance of privatization for Russian tripartism remains uncertain. On the one hand, in terms of managerial autonomy Russia's economy is coming to resemble more closely the European market economies from which the tripartite model was adopted. Russia's government, though it is still far more heavily involved in the economy than its European counterparts, could in principle begin to play more of a mediating role. On the other hand, Russia's managers are neither well organized nor for the most part interested in negotiating stable, long-term contracts with workers, both necessary elements of successful tripartism. And the fundamental problems of shaky legitimacy and inability to achieve nationwide penetration still plague labor organization. The Tripartite Commission continues to function, but it is considered of marginal significance by informed observers.

Unions' Political Alliances and Electoral Role

Electoral politics provides another avenue for trade union influence over social, economic, and labor policy. In Europe unions have historically

sought such influence through formal alliances with labor, social democratic, Communist, and Christian democratic parties. In the United
States, the AFL-CIO's Committee on Political Education works to elect
candidates sympathetic to labor's interests, as do local- and state-level
unions.[15] Tentative moves toward union-party linkages began in Russia
during 1992. Aside from the aforementioned alliances between the FNPR
and Civic Union, Sotsprof and the Social Democratic Party of Russia,
other independents also maintained contacts with the Social Democrats,
and at least one of that party's factions developed ties to reformers within the FNPR who were trying to democratize.[16] The Party of Labor, led
by the well-known socialist intellectual Boris Kagarlitsky, gained the support of the FNPR's Moscow regional federation as well as other branch
unions. Each of these parties claimed to represent the interests of workers in their election campaigns.

    But the political system was still in formation: the parties proved
transient or weak, and none of the alliances held through the first genuine
multiparty election in December 1993. The Party of Labor remained tiny
and marginal. The Social Democrats, heavily factionalized around a few
party luminaries, failed to become a political force. The Civic Union, a
centrist bloc dominated by enterprise managers, split in 1993 and lost
the constituent party with the largest mass and blue-collar membership,
Nikolai Travkin's Democratic Party of Russia. Initiatives by prominent
Social Democratic Party, Labor Party, and FNPR leaders to form a left-
centrist/laborite bloc in the run-up to the election also failed because
the parties could not reach agreement.[17] In the event no serious social
democratic or left-centrist party even fielded candidates.

    For the election both the FNPR and independent unions fragmented
and dispersed their support across most of the dozen or so serious con-
tending parties. The FNPR's national leadership, caught in the midst of a
transition and chastened by charges that it had played too political a role
in the October 1993 conflict between Yeltsin and the parliament, chose to
keep a low profile and made no endorsements. It ignored overtures from
Gennady Zyuganov's Communist Party of the Russian Federation, self-
described as "the party of the working people." Some of the constituent
unions played a more active role. The trade unions of the agroindustrial
complex, the largest in the FNPR, supported the Agrarian Party, with former
FNPR chairman Klochkov running as a candidate on that party's election
list. The Agrarians were antireform, supporting private land ownership
restrictions, employment guarantees, subsidies, and protectionist policies
for agriculture as well as for the related food processing and manufacturing sectors. They performed unexpectedly well in the election, placing

fourth with approximately 10 percent of the vote and giving the agro-industrial unions a potential voice in parliament.[18] FNPR-affiliated unions of the forestry sector, construction, and building materials unions supported the Civic Union, which was more moderately antireform and promised to minimize unemployment and regulate markets. The Civic Union performed abysmally, though, receiving less than 5 percent of the vote.[19] Some local unions of the FNPR supported other parties or candidates of their own selection. The Federation's passivity and disunity cost it any chance of commanding influence through the election.

The independent unions divided their support among more or less proreform candidates. Early in the campaign several independents tried unsuccessfully to create a proreform bloc so that they could run their own candidate list. Failing this they split. The Independent Miners' Union endorsed the party most closely identified with Yeltsin, Gaidar's Russia's Choice. Staunchly proreform, it promised austerity policies that would lower inflation, but it did not otherwise address the costs of reform for workers; it placed first in the election's outcome. The Air Traffic Controllers' Union supported Democratic Russia, itself split internally over policies and alliances. Sotsprof allied with Sergei Shakrai's Party of Russian Unity and Accord, which called for greater regional autonomy from Moscow, more gradual reform, and more attention to social welfare.[20] Divided, these unions were too small to provide significant electoral support for the parties they endorsed.

In any case, available evidence indicates that unions exercised little influence over their members' votes. Polls show that workers voted in significant numbers for Vladimir Zhirinovsky's right-wing, nationalist Liberal Democratic Party (LDP) and the Communist Party, both more extremist than any endorsed by the unions (though the Agrarians are not very distant in their politics from the Communists) and both stunningly successful in the elections, placing second and third respectively after Russia's Choice. Unemployed workers were more likely than others to vote for the Communist Party, which favors a strong regulatory role for the state as well as social protections.[21] The LDP's economic policies were not antireform but more nuanced—an economic nationalism combining continued development of the private sector with a more aggressive export strategy, especially for arms, and protection against foreign imports for Russian products. Zhirinovsky's support seems to have been stronger among older, less well educated, blue-collar workers, themselves employed but working in sectors that had experienced layoffs and other negative effects of reform, as well as among some younger, skilled workers.[22] Even in coal mining districts, where the NPG was influential, many ignored the union's endorsement of Russia's Choice to support Zhirinovsky. In the Kuzbass basin, for example, 25 percent of the vote went to the LDP.[23] Fewer than 9 percent of those in a large interview sample said that the trade union at their workplace had supported a bloc or candidate.[24]

Unions remained divided and ineffectual in the most recent elections. In the 1995 Duma election the FNPR's leadership for once did take a position, after several false starts. During the months leading up to the vote the Federation made a succession of alliances and tactical moves. In May it formed an electoral bloc with the Russian Unified Industrialists' Party (ROPP), which represented managers, and the Union of Realists. In June the FNPR created its own electoral association, Russian Trade Unions—Election Bound. In July it signed an agreement to join Ivan Rybkin's left-center bloc. In August it withdrew, reportedly because of dissension among regional affiliates. Finally, in September the FNPR formed the Trade Unions and Industrialists of Russia—Labor Alliance with the ROPP, which gained 1.5 percent of the popular vote (slightly more than 1 million votes) and won no seats. There was evidence of considerable division within the Federation over election strategy, especially between central and regional organizations. Many of the latter ultimately supported the Agrarians, the Communists, or the nationalist and vaguely socialist Congress of Russian Communities, which counted Aleksandr Lebed as one of its leaders.[25] Communist leader Zyuganov appealed for the support of regional organizations over Shmakov's head, with some success. In the critical 1996 presidential election, which pitted Zyuganov against Yeltsin, the FNPR apparently made no endorsement.

The independent unions were divided into two confederations by the time of the campaign for Duma elections. The Confederation of Russian Labor (KTR) took no position in the elections. The unions from the All-Russian Confederation of Labor (VKT) split their support. The NPG nominated its own candidates for Rybkin's bloc, with its chair, Aleksandr Sergeev, on the federal ticket. Sotsprof chair Sergei Khramov supported the small For Motherland Party, while his deputy joined the progovernment party of Prime Minister Chernomyrdin, Our Home Is Russia. Mining and Metallurgical Workers' Union chair Boris Misnik supported the proreform party Yabloko and won a seat in the Duma.[26] In the presidential election the independent unions generally supported Yeltsin but did not manage to make a collective endorsement. One observer aptly commented, "In the final analysis the campaign efforts of the [successor and independent] unions have resulted only in the dispersion of the defenders of [labor's] economic interests across the whole political spectrum."[27]

CHAPTER 4

PRIVATIZATION AND THE STATUS OF LABOR

The past few years have seen a massive change in the formal status of Russia's labor force: a large majority—more than 75 percent of industrial workers—many of them state employees as recently as 1993, now work at privatized enterprises and organizations in which most are also shareholders or part-owners (see Figure 4.1, page 66). The state's privatization program, administered by Anatoly Chubais's Committee for the Management of State Property (GKI), was applied first to small-scale service establishments such as retail stores and restaurants, then to medium- and large-scale industrial enterprises in most sectors of the economy. Privatization divested the state of ownership rights and responsibilities over Russia's vast economy in an extremely brief period, transforming most enterprises into privately owned joint-stock companies to be run by their own boards of directors. Much of the stock, however, remains in the hands of "insiders," managers and workers at the enterprises who were able to buy a controlling block of shares. Most small-scale establishments were also acquired by insiders through employee buyouts and other means. Meanwhile, an estimated 10 percent of Russia's labor force has moved into newly created private firms owned by entrepreneurs and outside investors.[1]

PRIVATIZATION OF INDUSTRY

The original intent of the Russian government's privatization program was to transfer control over most of Russia's 25,000 large and medium-sized industrial enterprises to new, entrepreneurial owners who would be driven by market criteria of efficiency and profitability. The reformers

Figure 4.1
Cumulative Percentage of Industrial Workforce in
Private and Privatized Enterprises*

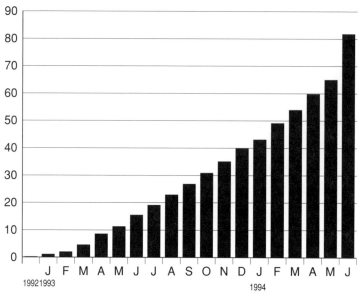

* Workers in medium- and large-scale industrial enterprises
Note: The unusually large increase in June 1994 is explained by the fact that the
first, voucher-based stage of privatization was scheduled to end on July 1, 1994.
Source: Russian Economic Trends, Monthly Update, April, 22, 1996, Statistical
Annex, Table 12 (no page).

saw such new owners as key to Russia's transition to a market-oriented
society: they would presumably have the managerial skills, technological
know-how, money, and willingness to carry out a successful if painful
restructuring of enterprises, including retooling, cutting labor forces,
seeking new markets, and so forth. The reformist government also wanted to halt the ongoing spontaneous or "nomenklatura" privatization,
through which managers and others from the old power structure were
acquiring de facto ownership over enterprises by illegal and semilegal
means. Chubais's initial program envisioned selling or auctioning the
majority of shares in enterprises to "outsiders," either foreign or domestic, who would acquire them through open and competitive bids.
Chubais's proposal also gave managers and workers a limited stake in
the process, granting them 25 percent of nonvoting shares in their company for free and additional shares on favorable terms.

   The plan to transfer control over Russian enterprises to outsiders
met with intense opposition from management and labor organizations.

To put the matter simply, managers and workers feared that they would be displaced in a takeover by new, market-minded owners. Moreover, many managers felt entitled to ownership rights in exchange for careers spent running their establishments, while many workers considered the factories as collective property that had been accumulated through their labor. Both groups thought it unjust to sell large parts of Russia's economy to foreigners or to newly rich Russians who had in many cases accumulated their wealth through corruption or political connections. This attitude was broadly shared among Russian society.

Managers' organizations mobilized rapidly against the threat to their interests and positions, condemning the government's privatization plan as an attempt to "break the spine" of the Russian directors' corps.[2] Managers would have liked to make straightforward claims of their own, but such an approach would have been isolating and politically inadvisable, especially given the pervasive charges of nomenklatura privatization and concerns about the justice of property distribution. Instead they chose an approach that would have broader appeal and attract support from worker and leftist constituencies, proposing that ownership be offered to the enterprise's entire "labor collective"—that is, all employees, labor and managerial—through a variety of buyout and employee stock ownership schemes. The FNPR took a similar position, insisting that enterprises should be transferred to their labor collectives at no or nominal cost. Labor and management formed an effective alliance to defend insiders' privileges; Volsky's Russian Union of Industrialists and Entrepreneurs coordinated with the leadership of the FNPR to press for worker-management buyouts and the exclusion of newcomers and foreigners from share ownership. Both lobbied their allies in the Supreme Soviet, which had to approve the final privatization program. The independent unions, though they agreed with the FNPR on little else, also supported the transfer of property rights to their members. The concept of privatization through transfer to the labor collective also had considerable support throughout Russian society, though many argued that citizens not working in the goods-producing sector (for example, teachers and doctors) were also entitled to a share in Russia's wealth.[3]

The privatization program approved by the Supreme Soviet in June 1992 is broadly regarded as a victory for the managers' lobby. It made critical concessions to the pressures from management and labor, offering a second privatization plan (Option 2) that allowed members of an enterprise's labor collective to obtain a minimal controlling share of stock, 51 percent, through closed subscription and without discount before any shares were sold to outsiders. Chubais's original plan, 25 percent of nonvoting shares distributed free to the labor collective with the option to buy an additional 15 percent at discount, was retained as Option 1.[4] In both cases, the remainder of the shares would be held temporarily by local and regional property funds set up for the purpose and later sold at auctions or on the secondary market. (A third option was also specified, but it was little used and need not be discussed here.) The legislation also provided that enterprises could put large portions of their profits and other incentive funds into employees' privatization accounts, easing managers' and workers' access to the resources necessary to buy a controlling share. In the summer of 1992 the government, responding to claims that everyone had some rights to the socialist state's property, distributed vouchers with a face value of 10,000 rubles at nominal cost to all Russian citizens. Most firms undergoing privatization were instructed to offer shares at voucher auctions once closed subscriptions had been completed. Some fourteen thousand large and medium-sized Russian enterprises were required or allowed to privatize under these options in 1992, and the number was increased to nineteen thousand by mid-1994, with some strategic sectors excluded.[5] Privatization proceeded rapidly, with a large majority of enterprises choosing Option 2.

Both the politics and process of privatization reinforced Russian workers' habit of looking to management to protect its interests. Managers' organizations led the parliamentary lobbying for insider control. On the shop floor managers used their old paternalistic stance, promising to "maintain the labor collective"—that is, continue to guarantee employment and social services after privatization—and encouraging workers in the (credible) belief that there was much to fear from an outside takeover. Once the complex process of privatization had begun, managers became the controllers of information and authoritative interpreters of the rules, guiding workers through the necessary decision points. Each enterprise first had to form a privatization commission and convert itself into a joint-stock company, of which the sitting director automatically became chair. It then had to select one of the three options, distribute shares internally, and deal with the local property committees that approved enterprises' plans, the property funds that auctioned off the remaining shares, and the stream of regulations and directives that supplemented the basic legislation.

Though they clearly held the upper hand, managers also needed the cooperation of their workers in order to secure control. Enterprise privatization commissions required labor representation, and if an effective commission did not appear within a specified time frame the GKI could come in and establish one. More important, the decision for the labor collective to purchase 51 percent of the stock (Option 2) required the approval of two-thirds of all employees; the collective could choose to acquire a smaller share on more favorable terms (Option 1), or, if it failed to reach a decision, the GKI could impose Option 1 by default. Though workers generally had their own reasons to prefer Option 2, any conflict at the factory could disrupt the privatization process and trigger state intervention detrimental to managers' interests. This created a strong incentive for managers to minimize friction in labor relations by avoiding layoffs, restructuring, and other measures, at least until privatization was completed. Workers' and managers' interests in consolidating insider property rights were thus intertwined, encouraging dependence and cooperation (however calculating and mutually distrustful) between the two rather than the development of workers' independent organizing capacity and collective action on behalf of their interests.

Despite this induced cooperation with labor, by most accounts managers used the privatization process as a pretext to weaken further and marginalize unions—even the FNPR unions that were closely tied to management. A 1993 survey at enterprises in Moscow, Stavropol *krai* (district), Nizhniy Novgorod, and Tyumen oblast that had been converted to joint-stock companies found that "in reality collectives do not participate [in privatization] . . . everything is decided by the enterprise administration and central and local bodies of authority"; it concluded that "trade unions as institutions of collective management have lost even their past minimal influence on the process of making principally important decisions."[6] The chairman of the Tatar Republic FNPR council complained of attempts to belittle trade unions' role and eliminate (illegally) their rights in the privatization process. FNPR chair Klochkov condemned the sometimes successful efforts by enterprise directors to break up or ban trade unions in the newly formed joint-stock companies.[7] The independent unions characteristically took a stronger stance, but their disputes tended to be with state authorities. The Pilots' Union, for example, threatened to strike when the GKI challenged the pilots' right to hold 51 percent of shareholder equity in Moscow's Sheremetyevo International Airport, while the St. Petersburg Seaport Workers formed a strike committee to oppose the prospect of "rich outsiders" buying or leasing equipment at the seaport.[8]

By the end of 1993 more than three-fourths of eligible Russian industrial enterprises had been privatized, with 79 percent of enterprise collectives selecting Option 2. Workers were able to use vouchers as well as their firms' profit and incentive funds to buy shares, which were in any case cheap because their price was not adjusted for the soaring inflation in 1992 and 1993. In addition to the 51 percent of shares bought via closed subscription, workers and managers typically acquired additional shares—sometimes as much as 15–20 percent more—at voucher auctions, which they usually dominated. Some 17 percent of labor collectives chose Option 1. Most were from poor enterprises in light industry such as textiles, whose labor collectives lacked the financial resources to purchase stock and preferred to take for free the 25 percent offered by the state.[9] Voucher funds and other domestic investors also bought shares, but few of the feared foreign investors materialized. Most foreign businessmen were simply not interested in Russia's outdated industrial infrastructure, especially since the potentially lucrative oil and gas sectors were not on offer at this stage of privatization. The process produced a strong pattern of insider ownership. Various surveys showed that, at the end of the first stage of privatization, workers and managers together owned an average of 70 percent of shares in enterprises privatized under Option 2; managers alone owned an estimated 15–20 percent, though the averages for all privatized enterprises were lower.[10]

The second, postvoucher stage of privatization during 1994–96 saw some redistribution of ownership, with both managers and outside investors increasing their shares while the average stake of rank-and-file workers fell. Russian banks and investment funds constituted the bulk of outside investors. Still, the overall pattern of insider dominance held, with various surveys concluding that insiders owned the majority of stock in 65 percent of medium- and large-scale enterprises while outsiders were majority owners in less than 20 percent (the remainder having no majority owner).[11] The vast preponderance of stockholders remained rank-and-file employees, but their average collective share fell, according to one study, from 53 percent in December 1994 to 43 percent in June 1995, with an ongoing downward trend into 1996.[12] At the same time managers increased their shares and contrived to acquire large, concentrated stakes in a growing number of enterprises.[13]

Workers were often willing to sell their stocks because they saw no financial or other benefit to holding shares: most firms paid no dividends in the first year or two; any dividends paid were devalued by inflation; and workers often understood little about the potential for future earnings. Many sold because they were desperate for cash after months of unpaid wages. There were occasional charges that managers withheld wages in order to induce such sales. Managers sometimes brought in consignments of consumer durables to tempt workers to liquidate their stocks, offered prices well above the market, and set up stock-purchasing operations conveniently within the enterprise. Some engaged in subterfuges or manipulations during or after privatization to accumulate ownership, including creating commercial ventures, borrowing from banks, appropriating state subsidies and conversion funds, and establishing their own investment funds to buy shares on the secondary market.[14] Some fought the influence of outside stockholders by issuing additional stock to dilute the ownership pool. In sum, managers concentrated their resources on shoring up both ownership and control over enterprises.

LABOR IN THE POSTPRIVATIZATION ECONOMY

Does their new status as substantial shareholders give Russia's workers influence over decisionmaking in their enterprises? Perhaps under the present ownership structure shareholders' meetings or enterprise councils could serve as alternatives to trade unions, giving workers a voice in production and labor issues as well as some capacity to constrain managers. This would mean a mode of representation for Russia's workers very different from that of most of their Western counterparts, and it would raise questions about the usefulness of Western-style trade unions. Indeed, a number of analysts have voiced concerns about the influence accruing to workers in privatized enterprises, arguing that worker ownership may present obstacles to restructuring, especially to labor force cuts. One careful scholar of postprivatization companies speculated that, at least initially, "Management had little incentive to restructure . . . because far-reaching restructuring programs, which might jeopardize job security, are likely to endanger managements' chances in elections at shareholder meetings where employees are majority shareholders."[15]

Case studies and other evidence reveal, however, that managers remain firmly in control of most privatized enterprises. Managers are often able to control placement on boards of directors and shareholder councils and are almost always able to dominate their agendas. After examining the potential for workers' influence on boards of directors, the authors of a large-scale study of postprivatization enterprises concluded:

> Theoretically, groups of workers and their trade unions could have meaningful independent power on these company boards. As large blockholders in their own right, they could nominate their own candidates and use cumulative voting to elect them. They could choose respected lawyers, public figures, or business people to represent their interests on the board. Yet we have not recorded one case in which they did so. These findings reflect the fact that Russian trade unions are

heavily dominated by management. . . . In what free market
economy could workers in most large factories belong to trade
unions, own the majority of their companies' shares, yet never
elect an independent representative to the board of directors?
. . . Now the managers rule supreme.[16]

As a consequence, decisions about changes in production lines and
organization, job assignments, and the like remain with management.
At the Pionerka clothing factory, for example, management initiated all
business in the shareholders' council and decided unilaterally on a series
of changes in production and efforts to tighten labor discipline. At the
Plastmass Chemical Factory senior managers and shop chiefs dominated the board of directors and carried out a reorganization that reduced
the labor force by more than one-third.[17] In many other cases as well,
worker ownership has provided no protections against labor force cuts
and changes in compensation procedures imposed unilaterally by management. Even where successful postprivatization transition programs
have raised wages and expanded labor forces, worker-owners have played
a subordinate and dependent role.[18]

There remains the question of how privatized enterprises will
behave, whether they will pursue market-oriented strategies as the
reformers intended. Many economists argue that insider ownership, whether by managers or workers, will block enterprises' adaptation to the market because such players do not have the necessary
abilities, resources, and incentives. They point out that the old,
Soviet-era managerial cadre, which remains in place as directors
(and now as elected presidents of the new boards of directors in
most cases), lacks the education and entrepreneurial skills necessary to become efficient, competitive, and profitable. Moreover, the
privatization process, in which enterprises were purchased mainly
with their own profits and government-issued vouchers, generated little of the new funds needed for plant restructuring and mod-
ernization. The dominance of insider ownership means further that
there will be only a minority of independent shareholders, who
dominate in Western corporations, demanding profits and thereby
imposing financial discipline on managers. Capital and stock markets are in any case too poorly developed to respond to company
performance. All these missing elements—managerial talent,
financing, external pressures for accountability—could have helped
advance reform at a time when Russian managers must make some
adaptations to the loss of their traditional suppliers and markets,

and to the large cuts in government subsidies that have followed privatization, if their enterprises are to survive.

Scattered empirical findings show that managers have in practice pursued a wide variety of strategies in the postprivatization economy. Though not all are market-oriented, they often have involved substantially overhauling production and redeploying or shrinking the labor force. Some managers have been able to rely on political connections to get state contracts, subsidies, or scarce export licenses for their goods. The manager of the Pionerka clothing factory, for example, saved his ailing enterprise (which had been closed down temporarily) by getting a large contract to produce military uniforms, with guaranteed supplies and some subsidies for the necessary new equipment, and reorganized the shops accordingly. Others, such as the manager of the massive Plastmass Chemical Factory, have rationalized and streamlined production, cutting out inefficient lines and radically reducing the bloated payroll. Still others have engaged in asset stripping, transferring profitable industrial lines to subsidiary enterprises under their ownership, or liquidating production in order to lease enterprise premises. Managers at the LenKon Industrial Equipment Plant, for instance, transferred part of production from their centrally located facility to a lower-wage, rural district and cut the workforce in apparent preparation to lease plant buildings to foreign companies that would pay high, hard-currency rents.[19]

In fact, managers are largely uncontrolled, as the kinds of corporate legal frameworks and financial sanctions that constrain Western managers remain very weak in Russia. The potential for corruption and self-enrichment through expropriation of financial and other assets is great, and there are many examples involving both managers and officials. According to an authoritative report in *Ekonomika i Zhizn'*, the privatization process has included many cases of understating the book value of facilities slated for privatization, collusion of government officials in the illegal transfer of property, and deliberate violations of the procedures for organizing competitive bidding sessions and auctions. Officials in several regions have been prosecuted in criminal court for taking bribes and other abuses.[20] Corruption and irregularities in the redistribution of state property have become major political issues in the Russian Federation.

Under these circumstances, Russia's workers need effective, independent trade unions more than in the past to protect their interests. Restructuring seems unavoidable; industries that fail to adapt will simply cease functioning and furlough their workers at nominal pay. Moreover, the process has already begun at many enterprises, largely under the unilateral control of managers who reassign, lay off, and replace workers and change production organization and wage payment schemes at their discretion. Unions should not attempt broad resistance to this process but should press for restructuring strategies that will minimize the costs for workers and act as a check on managerial arbitrariness. Unions are needed to verify that staff reductions are technically justified, orderly, and respect seniority and other contractual protections, to bargain over the reorganization of production, and to try to block managers' asset-stripping strategies and make transparent their deals with commercial partners and investors. FNPR-affiliated unions have, as far as can be determined from available reports, on the whole been unwilling or unable to perform these functions effectively. At LenKon, the trade union simply endorsed dismissals by shop chiefs that targeted women, older workers, and those disliked by the administration; at the Bratchenko coal mine, it did not protest when the administration dismissed workers and brought in replacements. In instances where unions did protest, they made little headway.[21] In most cases the FNPR unions have been too closely tied or too long subordinated to management to make a strong, independent response.

The formation of independent unions may be more likely in the postprivatization economy than in earlier stages of reform. Though many constraints continue to militate against their development, some of the recent changes may be conducive to it. Most important is that paternalistic relations are beginning to break down at many enterprises. Provision of social benefits such as housing and day care by the employer is declining; some services are being transferred to municipalities during privatization. In some cases managers have taken housing built for the labor force and sold it on the free market at prices workers cannot afford.[22] Salary differentials between managers and workers have widened dramatically. Managers who in the past would have retained their workers, on unpaid leaves if necessary, have begun to fire them. As the enterprise protects and provides for workers less, they may be jolted into a clearer consciousness of their independent interests. Restructuring has brought a slight increase in the level of labor-management conflict and, as has been seen, some intensification of strike movements and militancy. Despite the high levels of worker share ownership, privatization also brings the position of Russia's workers closer to that of their Western counterparts: workers must now bargain not with the state but with managers who face, if not hard budget constraints, at least real economic pressures. Thus, the experience of Western unions should become increasingly relevant.

DEVELOPMENT OF THE NEW PRIVATE SECTOR

A new private sector, founded and run by entrepreneurs and private investors, has also taken shape in Russia. One of Mikhail Gorbachev's first economic initiatives was to legalize private economic activity with the 1986 Law on Individual Labor Activity, followed up by the 1988 Law on Cooperatives.[23] Though those seeking to establish new businesses have confronted severe problems with access to licenses, financing, and premises, as well as high taxes and pressures from organized crime, the private sector has made impressive gains. By the fall of 1995 it encompassed some 900,000 new businesses and employed about 15 percent of the labor force. Statistics on such companies are, however, poor: informed economists consider these estimates too low because much private activity goes unreported to evade taxation. Private businesses are concentrated in the service sector and have experienced their most dynamic growth in the areas of commerce and finance, where commodity exchanges, investment funds, insurance companies, and banks have proliferated. Small, private manufacturing enterprises have also grown up rapidly and now provide more than 10 percent of industrial employment.[24] Petty economic activities such as farming small plots, driving taxis, tutoring, and selling consumer goods, food, and personal possessions in markets, at train stations, and on the streets are also engaging large numbers of people.

From the perspective of this study the private sector is important for two reasons. For one, it is almost entirely nonunionized. The FNPR never gained a foothold, and independents have made few inroads. Unions of cooperative workers have emerged, but these are trade associations rather than true labor unions. Private businesses attract workers by offering greater prestige and much higher wages than those normally paid in the state sector or in newly privatized industries, but workers have few protections of any kind. Social services and benefits are generally not provided; safety violations are rampant; hiring and firing is at the discretion of managers; and sexual harassment of women is reportedly common.[25] Yet the prospects for successful organizing seem poor. Those engaged in international assistance to Russian unions should provide particular encouragement to organizing initiatives in this area. Though managers are likely to be hostile, organizers can count on certain advantages: the FNPR poses no obstacle to new unions; there is no tradition of paternalism; and the structure of labor-management relations in the entrepreneurial outfits most closely resembles the Western pattern.

The private sector also functions to absorb some of the workers dismissed from older industries. Skilled and motivated workers who find their wages and hours cut can move into the private sector even as the overall demand for labor falls. Others will need retraining, and programs that teach them skills useful for work in the rapidly expanding commercial economy will be most useful. While job retraining programs in the West have had limited success, the drastic shortage of commercial skills in Russia's economy means that such retraining will likely produce higher rates of new employment in the private economy there.[26]

CONCLUSION

In considering the potential for trade union organization, certain unexpected features of the postprivatization Russian economy must be noted. The majority of Russian enterprises have not adjusted to the market and continue to limp along because there are no effective bankruptcy laws. At these enterprises, workers produce little and receive no wages, but neither are they unemployed or cut off from enterprise social benefits. Instead, many managers, motivated by a combination of paternalism, expectations that production will increase, and continuing hopes for federal subsidies, keep workers who would be fired in a true market economy. Further, though enterprises have cut back on their provision of social services and transferred some to local governments, these cuts have been far more modest than might be expected, affecting perhaps 10–20 percent of services and related expenditures. Thus, large numbers of workers continue to live in enterprise-owned housing, retain access to medical and child care, and eke out a living through occasional wages, barter, and subsidiary production (mainly small-scale farming) . These workers could not credibly threaten to withhold their labor since much of it is superfluous anyway. Nor could they demand more from enterprises that are, in many cases, virtually bankrupt. It is difficult to imagine how they could be organized into traditional trade unions.

Perhaps typical are people such as Mikhail and Galina Razzhivins, a couple in their thirties, with four children, who worked at a defense plant in the small industrial town of Nerekhta. Both were sent on extended leave from the plant when it underwent conversion to the production of civilian goods and have neither worked nor received wages for months. However, both are still employees of the enterprise and they continue to receive benefits from it. The children attend its summer camp, while the parents spend their time growing and canning vegetables from a one-acre plot. There are few other jobs available in Nerekhta, where the defense plant employed a third of all workers.[27] The couple's passive acceptance of the situation is reinforced by paternalism and by the possibility for petty private activity. They do not conceive of organization or collective action as part of the solution to their problems.

CHAPTER 5

WESTERN AID TO RUSSIA'S TRADE UNIONS

POLICY ASSESSMENT AND PRESCRIPTION

Russian workers need trade unions that can effectively negotiate the costs of the current economic transition for the labor force; work to distribute the burden of those costs more evenly among different strata of society, in order to curb the rapid growth of income disparities and the rise in the numbers of the working poor; provide oversight to improve the transparency of the privatization process and enterprise finances and to limit managerial arbitrariness; and press for an adequate safety net to cushion the impact of growing unemployment and to sustain needed social services that are being dropped by privatized enterprises. At present, Russia's unions, independent or successor, can accomplish none of these tasks. Reform has brought a substantial and sustained decline in real wages and has plunged almost one-fourth of the population below the poverty line. At present, wages are in arrears more often than not and commonly go unpaid for weeks and months at a time. Managers regularly violate labor legislation, refusing to recognize new unions, ignoring collective bargaining agreements, and dismissing workers arbitrarily despite seniority and other rules. Government likewise fails to pay wages to workers or its debts to industry and regularly ignores the agreements it has negotiated with unions at the national level. Many unions have been marginalized through the privatization process, which left managers more firmly in control and increased their incentive to rid their enterprises of expensive benefit provisions. Large numbers of workers face further, painful restructuring of their sectors and layoffs in the absence of adequate unemployment insurance or job referral networks. Unions have tried to defend their members through collective bargaining, industrial action, lobbying, and participation in the Tripartite Commission, but their successes have been very few.

In short, Russia's unions are weak, and the prognosis for their evolving into self-sustaining institutions that can defend the interests of the labor force is at best guarded. If such a development is to take place, four major changes are necessary:

1. The independent unions must acquire the resources and skills to retain and expand their membership. They need a legislative and institutional environment that evens their chances to recruit with the FNPR; namely, social insurance funds must be placed firmly under government administration, and rights of all unions to bargain collectively for their members must be guaranteed. The independents also need access to technical and economic expertise in order to negotiate with management over the future of their enterprises. Further, they must cease destructive infighting at the national level and join forces if they are to exercise any influence on policy in Moscow. Even granting them the most promising scenario, however, the independents are too few, and their growth has been too lackluster, to expect that they will come to represent more than a small part of the labor force. On the other hand, any expansion will increase the pressures for reform on the union grouping to which most workers still belong, the FNPR.

2. The FNPR must democratize, turning its substantial resources to the genuine defense of its members and establishing its independence from management. The FNPR alone has in place the organization, trained personnel, and financial, technical, and other resources necessary to function as a nationwide promoter of labor's interests. It must stop relying mainly on its eroding role as distributor of managerial largesse to retain members, confront the fact that managerial and labor interests are increasingly divergent in the postprivatization economy, and work to build authority and legitimacy among its rank and file through elections and other accountability mechanisms. If it does not democratize, the FNPR is likely to face diminished relevance, continual defections, and survival mainly as a quasi-commercial organization.

3. The legislative, institutional, professional, and normative bases for trade union organization and collective bargaining must become firmly ingrained. As preceding chapters have argued, a large part, though not all, of the legislative basis is already in place. Now the legal system must be developed in the area of labor relations. New

institutions for arbitration and enforcement of collective bargaining agreements must be put into place. A cadre of labor and public
interest lawyers must be trained. Unions and workers must be
informed of their rights and must have the resources to seek redress.
Norms will be changed only slowly, through day-to-day practice.

4.   The Russian government must begin to deal in good faith with the
      unions. The government since Boris Yeltsin took firm control, has
      created national bargaining mechanisms and proceeded to treat
      them with disdain, ignoring agreements reached and playing politics
      with unions' rights to representation. Such contemptuous official
      treatment further undermines already weak unions as well as the
      credibility of those in positions of power. The government should
      bargain in good faith or not at all and should promise to labor only
      what it is willing and able to deliver. At both the central and munic-
      ipal levels it must also develop the administrative capacity to handle
      welfare services as unemployment rises and enterprises begin to
      abandon their traditional social responsibilities. Whether and to
      what extent these changes will take place depends mainly on devel-
      opments within Russia, but Western organizations can play a role.

U.S. AND OTHER WESTERN ASSISTANCE PROGRAMS

An overview of the major U.S. assistance programs, carried out by the
AFL-CIO's Free Trade Union Institute (FTUI), has already been provided
in the Introduction. Following is a more extended discussion of FTUI's
funding (see Table 5.1, page 82) and the components of the programs.[1]

MOSCOW AND LIAISON OFFICES

FTUI's Moscow field office was set up in the spring of 1992 under
the directorship of Thomas Bradley. Until this point the AFL-CIO's contacts had been almost exclusively with the NPG, and Bradley went into
what was described as a "difficult situation in which he had to do all the
groundwork"[2] to locate and make contacts with other independents. In
an interview during the spring of 1993, he gave the impression of a committed activist who had accumulated extensive knowledge about the size
and structure of independent unions as well as their problems. He listed
five critical needs for the growth of the independent union movement:

TABLE 5.1
FUNDING FOR FTUI's PROGRAMS IN THE
RUSSIAN FEDERATION

NED		AID	
1990	. . . .$300,000[a]	10/92–10/94	. . . .$1,190,000
1991	. . . . .1,000,000[a]	7/94–7/96	3,830,000
1992	1,000,000	4/96–97	. . . . .1,700,000[b]
1993	1,000,000		
1994	1,040,000		
1995	880,000		
1996	. . . . .417,500[b]		

[a] figure is for the whole of the USSR
[b] obligated

Source: Author interviews with Daniel Rosenblum, senior program officer for the former Soviet Union, Free Trade Union Institute, Washington, D.C., December 19, 1995, and August 29, 1996. For the most part, NED has funded the liaison offices, the Trade Union Organizers' and Interns' Programs, and *Delo*; AID has funded RAFTURE, the "Rule of Law" Project, and radio and television programming. The two have shared administrative costs.

organization, expertise, case precedents to make labor law enforceable, the breakup of the FNPR or at least its loss of control over social insurance funds, and a free trade union center to facilitate communication and cooperation among emerging independents.[3] By the end of Bradley's two-year tenure FTUI's educational, legal, and other programs had expanded significantly with the addition of AID funding and new personnel.

Bradley's successor, Scott Reynolds, institutionalized the office's relations with the major independent unions through monthly meetings with their leaders and the formation of an advisory council. FTUI also works with a broad range of other regional, local, and enterprise-based independents. FTUI documents describe a highly consultative process in which the independents have a considerable say in program planning and development.[4] Staff intend the Moscow office to serve as a "contact point" for independents' leaders, providing forums for communication and cooperation. They take some credit for recent moves toward unity, in particular the formation of the Confederation of Russian Labor (KTR) in April 1995 (which, however, soon split up in a conflict over leadership). FTUI program officer Daniel Rosenblum acknowledges that heavy infighting among leaders of the national independents continues, and that FTUI's most promising work is its outreach and support to regional union organizations that are more practical and willing to cooperate with one another.[5] FTUI staff report regular travel around Russia's regions to meet with leaders of new, often isolated, unions, to offer them services, and to put them in touch with established independents.

"RULE OF LAW" PROJECT

The "Rule of Law" Project funds three labor law centers staffed by approximately twelve Russian lawyers as well as student interns in Moscow, St. Petersburg, and Yekaterinburg; a fourth office in Vladivostok has been closed. The centers consult on issues involving labor and trade union rights, litigate cases, engage in legislative advocacy, and do training and outreach to independent unions and activists, all on a pro bono basis. Besides covering operational expenses (at a level of $500,000 for the eighteen-month period from August 1994 to December 1995), FTUI staff advise on running the offices and selecting cases.[6] The bulk of the centers' work involves hundreds of telephone consultations on a range of standard wage, benefit, and rights issues, particularly the much-noted problems with rampant payment arrears, layoffs and forced leaves without pay or severance, internal job transfers during restructuring, problems with union registration, and violations of collective bargaining agreements. Labor law center lawyers advise independent trade unions during collective bargaining, help prepare pamphlets on worker rights that have been distributed to a mailing list of five-hundred union-related organizations, and teach workshops on legal advocacy for union interns, activists, and officials.[7]

Center lawyers have litigated about fifty cases—half successfully—that were selected mainly for their significance in affirming the organizing and bargaining rights of new unions.[8] Most cases are argued on behalf of established or fledgling independents that confront illegal managerial obstruction, retaliation, or other abuses. For example, at the Avtodizel Factory in Yaroslavl the management refused to recognize the independent trade union and unlawfully withheld benefits from its chairman. A lawyer from the Moscow Labor Law Center represented the union in court, where its legal status was upheld. Management had to compensate the chairman and subsequently agreed to negotiate a collective bargaining agreement with the union.[9] Other cases involve illegalities and obfuscations during privatization, for instance, a case in which an enterprise illegally privatized workers' housing. Still others allege improperly withheld wages and wrongful dismissals. According to FTUI staff, court victories can function as an "organizing tool" for new unions, establishing their credibility and delivering some tangible benefits to their members.[10] They can also demonstrate unions' ability to make powerful managers comply with the law.

"Rule of Law" lawyers also engage in legislative advocacy. As Chapter 2 showed, a great deal of legislation on organized labor's basic rights has been passed recently by the Duma. FTUI reports describe labor law center lawyers as deeply involved in the legislative process, publishing critiques of draft laws, informing independents about the implications of these laws for their unions, supporting lobbying efforts, and maintaining contacts with governmental and legislative committees concerned with labor and social issues. Center lawyers have aided the lobbying activities of independents against legislation that would give the sole collective bargaining rights to the largest trade union at an enterprise—in almost all cases the FNPR. Moscow Center lawyers advised the pilots' union in a case involving the constitutionality of antistrike legislation and testified as expert witnesses in the Constitutional Court's hearing on the matter. The Court found a ban on strikes in transport and aviation to contradict the constitution's guarantee of a right to strike, though it did not uphold this right unconditionally.[11] This case illustrates how even a small program may influence critical decisions during the formative stage of Russian labor law. FTUI staff consider the "Rule of Law" program one of their most successful and have retained it in spite of the budget cuts, though planned expansion has been canceled.

TRAINING AND ORGANIZERS' AND INTERNS' PROGRAMS

Another major component of FTUI's aid effort is a program designed to transfer useful skills and knowledge from the American union context to independent trade unionists and activists through training seminars. Initially, focus was on getting union activists from all parts of Russia to go through a sequence of two three-day seminars on "Basic Unionism and Collective Bargaining" that covered such topics as principles, goals, and activities of free trade unions, membership recruitment, preparing for negotiations, enforcement of the collective bargaining agreement, and labor dispute resolution.[12] While these basic seminars still form the core of the program, some that are more specialized and tailored to the interests and needs of particular unions—like enterprise finances (how to read the books), political action (including the mechanics of effective political endorsement and mobilization), and problems of the mining sector—have been added. Seminars are conducted throughout Russia, with an estimated 2,100 Russian unionists having attended one by the fall of 1995.[13] Again, FTUI reports describe a process of regular consultation with the independents in both designing seminar content and selecting participants. Over time, FTUI's programs have increasingly stressed the development of an indigenous training capacity, or "training trainers," that is, assisting Russian unions in developing their own education specialists who can teach the seminars. The purpose is to create a "multiplier effect" that would spread these skills throughout the independent union movement, especially into regions far from Moscow, and so make the program sustainable without further American support.[14] The training program has also been retained after the budget cuts; the basic seminars are now taught exclusively by Russians, while the more advanced, though they still have some American participation, are being transferred as well.

The Trade Union Organizers' and Interns' Program was intended to strengthen recruitment and internal administration among Russian independents by paying the salaries of activists while they worked on the staffs of existing national unions (interns) or ran recruitment campaigns (organizers). Internships were temporary, staffed by low-level activists who had gone through FTUI training seminars; in 1994–95 there were about twenty-five working at any one time, receiving salaries of $250 monthly.[15] They provided membership services and legal advice, worked on collective bargaining agreements, among other responsibilities, in FTUI's view helping slightly to "level the playing field" between the resource-poor independents and the FNPR. Organizers—approximately twenty at the same salary—were initially sent into regions and sectors that lacked independent unions to conduct recruitment and registration campaigns.

Both programs soon sparked controversy. Critics charged that Russian unionists should not be on American payrolls, that such an arrangement would make the unions susceptible to the political influence and control of the United States rather than their own members. The organizers' component came in for particularly harsh criticism, including some from independents. There were accusations that the AFL-CIO was attempting to establish its own network of client unions in Russia, that its paid organizers were competing with the efforts of Russia's genuine independents, and that they sometimes used pressure tactics to produce the false appearance of results.[16] FTUI disclaimed any such motives,[17] but it revamped the organizers' portion of the program. Organizers are now attached to existing independent unions or regional federations and recruit on their behalf.[18] In the face of both criticisms and budget cuts, the interns' segment of the program was ended.

RAFTURE, COMMUNICATIONS, AND MEDIA PROJECTS

The Russian American Foundation for Trade Union Research and Education (RAFTURE) was the single largest component of FTUI's budget, funded by AID at a level of $1,065,000 for 1992–94 and $1,860,000 for 1994–96. It provided educational, research, and publishing services for other FTUI programs, produced a range of literature and publicity on the union movement, and sought to link the independents with sympathetic intellectuals and public figures. The literature sponsored by RAFTURE ranged from articles on labor issues written by a network of press correspondents for local papers, to practical brochures on organizing and legal issues, to academic studies on the sociology of the labor movement. Materials were sent, as in the case of the "Rule of Law" Project's labor law center pamphlets, to some five hundred organizations in an effort to keep independents informed about and connected to the broader labor movement. Representatives of independents sat on RAFTURE's Advisory Council and also, along with public figures and scholars, on its Joint Advisory Council, providing forums for leaders to meet with one another and to raise their political visibility. The foundation's first director, Pavel Kudiukin, was a well-known social democrat and former deputy labor minister. RAFTURE brought respected labor specialists to advise FTUI.[19] The project was ambitious but also expensive and amorphous. Except for its educational component it was eliminated in the recent budget cuts.

FTUI has also provided communications and office equipment to independent unions and sponsored a radio program and newspaper to publicize their activities as well as labor issues generally. The newspaper, *Delo*, was founded in late 1992, supported by a NED grant of $240,000 a year, and had correspondents in many Russian regions. Some independents expressed concern initially that it would compete with their own publications, and they were given small grants to cover any losses. The paper was run by professional journalists and distributed to trade unions in twenty cities through collective subscriptions, reportedly reaching a circulation of 60,000 copies.[20] *Delo* showed no tendency to become self-supporting, however, and its value to independents remained difficult to demonstrate. Its funding was suspended in early 1996. Funding for a radio program focusing on labor issues was cut in the spring of that year.

Programs by AFL-CIO Affiliates

Two AFL-CIO affiliates, the American Federation of Teachers (AFT) and the United Mine Workers of America (UMW), have run separate programs of assistance to their Russian counterpart unions. The AFT, working with a subgrant from FTUI, established the AFT Teacher Organizing and Education Resource Center in Moscow in 1993 to assist independent local teachers' unions and organizing initiatives among educators, as well as to promote civic education. In late 1994 the center sponsored a large National Conference on Civic Education to promote the use of a "democracy curriculum" in place of the old Marxist-Leninist dogma in Russian schools. It has run numerous specialized seminars on collective bargaining, union administration, and legal and educational issues for teachers' unions. Where independent local unions, such as the Free Professional Teachers' Union of St. Petersburg, had emerged, the AFT provided leadership training. It also ran tailored workshops on collective bargaining in higher education at universities with independent unions; for example, at Voronezh State University in early 1995 it ran a workshop to help a new union prepare for negotiation by critically working through the union's strategy, anticipating difficulties, and explaining in detail how such arbitration and other procedures work in the United States. Toward the end of the AFT's grant period in 1995 a broader independent educators' union, the Trade Union Federation of Higher Education Employees of Russia, was formed with AFT support, but it has not achieved national visibility. At the same time, the AFT was instrumental in blocking affiliation of the FNPR Education and Science Employees' Union of Russia (ESEUR) with the international secretariat of educational trade unions (EI). The AFT monitored ESEUR conferences and reported that administrators exercised much control over the unions' governing bodies; therefore it was deemed insufficiently democratic to qualify for membership in EI.[21]

The United Mine Workers also sponsors an assistance program, in conjunction with the U.S. Mine Health and Safety Administration, to promote union democracy and health and safety protection in Russian mines. Called Partners in Economic Reform (PIER), the program is separately funded and primarily runs seminars for Russian miners. It also provides the NPG with direct links to its American counterpart union, contributing to FTUI's broader efforts to promote such contacts.[22]

OTHER WESTERN ASSISTANCE

Other international and Western organizations also provide assistance to Russia's trade unions. The International Labor Organization runs educational and technical assistance programs for unions in eighteen countries, including the Russian Federation, through its Central and East European advisory team in Budapest. In Russia it has sponsored training courses and conferences on collective bargaining, health and safety, wages and employment, social security, and other issues, as well as running seminars and translating and providing materials for trade union educators.[23] In 1995 the ILO directed a large conference on privatization that covered the role played by collective bargaining in privatized enterprises in market economies, as well as the importance of consultation and involvement of workers' organizations in the privatization process. Another large seminar focused on occupational health and safety issues. Its overall budget for Russia in that year was $200,000. The ILO does collaborate with independent unions, but the bulk of its work is with the FNPR. It is presently planning a three-year project with senior staff of the FNPR's training institute, the Academy of Labor and Social Relations, to revitalize the union's education system, with a budget request of $500,000 for 1997. According to Pekko Aro, an official at the Budapest office, the ILO recognizes the value of the independents but sees the FNPR as potentially reformable. "Though much experience with the FNPR has been less than encouraging, many branch structures have become quite militant. The FNPR can come to see itself as an independent union in a market economy . . . in any case in terms of organizing representation of wage employees, one can't go around it."[24]

The ILO's approach differs markedly from that of FTUI. The ILO is committed to the tripartite bargaining structure, and it seeks to promote cooperation among labor, management, and government in resolving the problems of transition. It works with representatives of all three to enhance bargaining mechanisms as well as organizational and regulatory capacities. It has, for example, provided technical support and advice for the development of governmental labor inspection and employment services, reform of social protection, and drafting of labor legislation. It runs seminars on labor market adjustment strategies for representatives of government, employers, and labor, and it is preparing policy advisory services that will provide "best-practice examples" in limiting unemployment from the experiences of Western and Eastern Europe.[25] Its assistance to unions, in other words, is integrated with efforts to build up the governmental capabilities and employer organizations that might make tripartism workable.

The International Confederation of Free Trade Unions, an independent trade union organization that dominates the workers' side of the tripartite ILO structure, sponsors its own program of aid to Central and Eastern Europe, including Russia. The ICFTU runs a regionwide trade union rights project and has sponsored a series of conferences in Russia on social security, unemployment, and related topics, designed to bring unions together to develop a common position on these issues. It has also organized conferences at which union leaders meet with representatives of the World Bank and the International Monetary Fund (IMF), international lending agencies that have been heavily involved in the design of Russia's economic restructuring program, to focus on the social impacts of reform. The ICFTU works with both independent and FNPR unions. The head of the organization's coordinating unit for Central and Eastern Europe, said that her organization knew the shortcomings of the FNPR, but that the independents were too small and faced too many obstacles to have much impact. She also stressed the pressures on the FNPR to become more responsive to its members: "96 percent of organized workers belong to the FNPR. The neoliberal attack on workers' rights has affected all workers. Any trade union movement must respond."[26]

Finally, the Friedrich Ebert Institute runs a training and assistance program for Russian unions. Beginning in 1991 the Institute conducted seminars on organizational aspects and functions of trade unions in Western societies, initially for the benefit of the FNPR and later also for independent unions. The Ebert Institute has maintained dialogues with the various unions and sets up seminars or brings in advisers in response to perceived needs or opportunities to encourage reformist trends. It does not provide long-term legal support but would bring in an expert to advise on a specific problem that arose. The Ebert program is small, relying on one organizer, whose time is now shared with another program, and running twenty to thirty seminars per year in different parts of the country. Its activities peaked in 1994, then, like those of its U.S. counterpart, decreased because of funding cuts.[27]

ASSESSMENT OF THE AMERICAN EFFORT

THE RECIPIENTS' VIEW

In assessing the value and effectiveness of American assistance to Russia's trade unions it is natural to turn first to the recipients of that aid, leaders of Russia's independent unions. In a series of interviews,[28] principals of the major independents with which FTUI has worked were asked to evaluate the contribution of FTUI's programs: Were training seminars useful in membership recruitment and collective bargaining? Did labor law centers help the unions defend their legal rights? Did union leaders have input into program development? Were some programs more useful than others? Did FTUI facilitate or hinder cooperation among Russian unions? Interviews with aid beneficiaries may be expected to have some positive bias,[29] but they are the only means to get feedback from those directly involved in and affected by the programs. Moreover, the interviewees do show considerable variation in their evaluation of specific programs and in their overall response to FTUI's programs.

The major point to emerge from the interviews is that recipients valued most the programs that gave them concrete skills and information: the "Rule of Law" and training programs. Almost all praised the "Rule of Law" Project for providing critical information about labor rights, access to legal representation, and help in understanding and influencing legislative changes. For example, A. Shepel, vice-chairman of the Russian Trade Union of Dockers, said, "Of special significance are the legal programs, which teach concrete skills on how to participate in lawsuits. Especially for those who are directly involved in such activities: initiation of the suits, the hearings of the cases in court—all the relevant procedures."[30] L. Lerman, the otherwise critical vice chair of the Nizhegorodsky regional Sotsprof union, said, "The materials that are distributed by the Rule of Law Project . . . address different problems in the protection of workers' rights, in the collective labor contracts, etc. We often refer to these pamphlets in our work, and make good use of them . . . there are many interesting ideas in the interpretation of current legislation. . . . We even used these ideas as a basis for the suggestions we made on the revision of the Labour Code."[31] Several cited cases that had been won in court for their unions by labor law center lawyers. The pilots' union vice president pointed to useful consultations with labor law center lawyers on illegal dismissals after strikes. A. Kochurov of the pilots' union replied when asked about the impact of funding reductions, "The main program that should be preserved and developed by all means is the program on legal training of members of our regional organizations and their union leaders."[32]

The training programs on union organizing, collective bargaining, and other fundamentals were also evaluated positively by most leaders, again with stress on the value of concrete information. According to Sotsprof chair Sergei Khramov, "Most useful for us was the practical information—the case studies. This is what the Americans taught us. Also, of no less importance are the methodological techniques—how to write a pamphlet, to conduct a meeting of the union, to carry out negotiations."[33] Several noted that unionists who had been through seminars became more successful recruiters and could teach their skills to others, though they were skeptical that many could organize such seminars on their own and none except the NPG talked of such a possibility. Nuts-and-bolts information necessary for collective bargaining was also judged extremely useful; as V. Pivnov, vice president of the Federation of Air Traffic Controllers' Unions, said: "The seminar on auditing in which I took part was very useful. We were taught how and what kinds of documents we should use during those audits. For here is what happens . . . they [the managers] give you a pile of documentation . . . and you wonder what you have to do with it. That is why the knowledge of how you should proceed with the documents is essential."[34]

Unionists were less favorable toward other aspects of the program. They were divided on the usefulness of *Delo*; some felt that indigenous papers could have filled the role.[35] Most appeared unaware of the other media programs. Few seemed to have been directly involved with RAFTURE, and none mentioned the fostering of ties to the intelligentsia through it. Taken as a whole, the interviews suggest that FTUI's funding was to a certain extent misallocated, with too much money going to media and research programs that had amorphous goals and limited impact. To FTUI's credit, when faced with large budget cuts it retained precisely the legal and training programs that were seen as most valuable by the recipients. If it gets money to expand the program again, FTUI should avoid the tendency to try doing a little bit of everything and stay with these narrowed priorities.

Leaders of two of the unions were highly critical of FTUI. Significantly, they were from NPG and Sotsprof, the two largest and longest-established of the independents.[36] NPG leader Aleksandr Sergeev complained that FTUI "applied Western stereotypes to the Russian trade union movement" and asserted that his union could find its own lecturers and design its own seminars. He charged that the Trade Union Organizers' and Interns' Program had worked without the consent of the NPG's governing body and that FTUI played political favorites, helping only unions that support liberal economic reforms. But Sergeev's main problem seemed to be that FTUI had opposed his decision to leave the KTR, the confederation of independents finally established in April 1995, to set up a second labor confederation with Sotsprof and other regional organizations; according to him, "we were called 'splitters' in the newspaper *Delo*, and attempts were made through organizers and interns to exert influence on the position of other unions, which did not enter the

first confederation formed in April."[37] Sotsprof's Khramov, while acknowl-
edging the value of training and other programs, complained of conflicts
over the manner of choosing and funding of program participants, and
said that the financial dependence of his and other unions on FTUI had
caused divisions among the independents. Khramov was clearly dis-
gruntled about his organization's share of FTUI funding and the degree
of support for his union, as well as the Americans' attempts to play a role
in interunion politics.[38]

The criticisms of these two leaders suggest some conclusions:
However desirable it might be for the independents to establish a national coordinating center, FTUI should not try to micromanage relations
among them or to force unity. It is surely constructive for FTUI staff to
facilitate contacts among the independents by organizing meetings—many
gave it credit for doing so[39]—but more than this is both overstepping and
overpoliticizing its role and is bound to lead to counterproductive conflicts with ambitious leaders. In another vein, FTUI's aid programs are
better received by unions in their start-up phase and seem to have diminishing returns for better-established, longer-term recipients, who become
overly expectant and disappointed with the type and extent of assistance
they receive. The views of these two leaders contrasted sharply with those
from newer and smaller unions, which seemed genuinely to need and
appreciate the help. Assistance should be concentrated on them.

THE VIEW FROM WASHINGTON, D.C.

How have U.S. aid and democracy-building efforts in Russia been
viewed by American policymakers? Consider first some of the issues and
criticisms that led to the drastic, across-the-board cuts in 1996. The bulk
of aid moneys to Russia were allocated under the Freedom Support Act,
passed by Congress in 1992. Over the following years the projects funded under this act, especially those administered by AID, were subject to
a number of criticisms in Congress and in the broader policy communi-
ty. Critics claimed that the projects were often wasteful and flawed in
concept, that they failed to produce timely results, and that too much
money went to expensive U.S. consultants rather than to people on the
ground.[40] There were charges that AID often relied on people lacking language or area competence in Russia and Eastern Europe to administer its
programs.[41] Others argued that the programs relied too heavily on short-
term consultants rather than resident advisers, that they failed to draw
local partners into an active role in planning and implementing assistance,

and that they paid little attention to the sustainability of their efforts.[42] The new Republican majority in the 104th Congress, mindful of these criticisms, disillusioned with the pace of democratization in Russia and the war in Chechnya, suspicious of foreign aid, and eager to reduce spending, responded by slashing the AID budget for assistance to Russia, forcing a reduction in its contribution to FTUI. The story at NED was somewhat different. Among NED's four core grantees (FTUI, the International Republican Institute, the National Democratic Institute, and the Center for International Private Enterprise), FTUI had received a disproportionately large share of funds since the endowment's formation in 1983 because it had programs already on the ground; now a more conservative Congress carried out long-discussed plans to equalize those shares, which involved a 50 percent reduction in FTUI's funding.[43]

How should one assess FTUI's record in light of these criticisms? Most, though not all, of FTUI's programs have been judged modestly successful. The conclusions of a recent U.S. General Accounting Office report broadly coincide with this study's findings and the interview results: "Beginning in 1992, FTUI's direct support for unions, education, outreach, and information dissemination, and legal assistance programs have made varying contributions to the development of new, democratic labor unions. However . . . the research activities of RAFTURE and . . . a media project did not make significant contributions to either trade union development or worker rights."[44] As seen, most of the FTUI's funds go to people working directly with trade unions. The program is administered by resident advisers who stay at least a couple of years and relies very little on expensive, short-term consultants. The record on language and regional expertise is mixed, though most trade union representatives interviewed responded favorably when asked whether FTUI's staff understood the situation in Russia and their particular problems, and Washington office staff had considerable area competence.[45] FTUI also has a good record in drawing local partners into the planning and implementation of assistance. Most of the trade union leaders described extensive discussions with FTUI staff and depicted a genuinely collaborative approach in which their views were taken into account.[46] Finally, FTUI pays explicit attention to what Thomas Carothers describes as the oft-ignored "basic rules of development assistance—the concept of local capacity-building, for example, programs to 'train trainers' and the sustainability of assistance programs."[47] Particularly in its training programs, FTUI seeks to transmit basic skills to people who will stay.

PROMOTING DEPENDENCE AND DIVISIVENESS?

The American aid effort has raised other controversies about the AFL-CIO's role abroad. While FTUI has worked in Eastern Europe only since the 1980s, and in Russia only since 1990, the AFL-CIO has a much longer history of assistance to foreign trade unions, particularly in Latin America. There, in the 1960s and 1970s, the American Institute for Free Labor Development (AIFLD), an earlier analogue of FTUI, ran an AID-funded assistance program that was geared toward countering Communist influence in Latin American labor movements and was in practice undiscriminating in its hostility to nationalist, socialist, populist, and social democratic unions. Critics charged that AIFLD promoted divisions within Latin American labor, supported repressive, authoritarian regimes as long as they had good anti-Communist credentials, generally subordinated its activities to the interests of American business and to the cold war aims of U.S. foreign policy, and in some cases served as a cover for CIA operations in the region. Many of these charges were substantiated, and they led to conflicts within the AFL-CIO's leadership as well as some opposition from the rank and file.[48]

By the 1980s the orientations of both the AFL-CIO and AIFLD had shifted in the direction of greater ideological tolerance and a central commitment to democratic institution building abroad. There were numerous reasons for this: the new emphasis in U.S. foreign policy on support for human rights, the AFL-CIO's differences with the conservative Reagan administration both at home and overseas, and the declining fortunes of organized labor in the United States. Perhaps most important was the American unions' realization that only a strong international labor movement pushing toward better wages and working conditions everywhere could protect U.S. workers' rights in the emerging global labor market.[49] With these changes, in addition to the end of the cold war and the collapse of communism, much of the old ideological baggage has become irrelevant, and there is more consensus now within the AFL-CIO over its international role.[50]

But some of the old criticisms have been revived in the Russian context. FTUI's programs, for example, have raised questions about the United States promoting its favorites among Russia's unions and about the financial and political dependence of the unions the institute does aid. Some charge that FTUI is creating divisions within and further weakening Russia's labor movement by encouraging independents to compete with the FNPR and by rewarding unions that break away, such as the metallurgists, with assistance. Others claim that dependence on foreign assistance is inherently corrupting for a labor union, removing leaders from control of the rank and file. Some see more a political agenda, insisting that FTUI has used its economic leverage over the independents to buy their support for Yeltsin and the neoliberal economic policies the U.S. government favors. According to one of the harsher critics, "Among large numbers of Russian worker activists, the American unions now have a foul reputation for attempting to suborn union leaders, to split and demobilize the Russian labor movement, and to subordinate it to government policies that have already brought large numbers of workers to hunger and destitution."[51] The FNPR subscribes to many of these criticisms.

For the most part, these charges blame FTUI for what are actually indigenous developments. The Russian labor movement is divided mainly because there are real and serious conflicts of interest between the FNPR and the independent unions. When asked about FTUI's policy of no contact with the FNPR, pilots' union vice-chair Kochurov said, "We share this position. While the FNPR makes efforts to monopolize all labor union activity . . . we cannot imagine ourselves cooperating with it."[52] Vice President Pivnov of the Federation of Air Traffic Controllers' Unions similarly replied, "It is we who do not want to have any relationship with the FNPR."[53] The metallurgists left the FNPR because they disagreed with the leadership's policies and wanted more control over their own resources.[54] As has been demonstrated in this paper, the independent unions adopted proreform positions long before they had contact with FTUI, and they have supported democratic candidates because they see their only hope for survival in the advancement of legal and institutional reform. The issue of dependence is a legitimate one, but the independents face such an uphill battle against entrenched forces that many would not survive to become self-sustaining organizations without outside help; as Pivnov affirmed, "We tried to organize our union on our own, but this needs help, technical and financial."[55] The solution is to make it clear from the outset that the aid will be short-term in nature and that unions must progressively take over the functions initially performed through outside assistance.

Whether FTUI should continue to focus its efforts almost exclusively on the independents remains a serious question. A number of arguments may be made in favor. According to Thomas Carothers, who has done extensive research on the subject, "democracy assistance . . . is most effective when it seeks to help people and organizations that already are trying to move in a democratic direction. . . . It cannot for the most part substitute for or create a will to reform that does not already exist."[56] The independents are clearly more democratic organizations than FNPR. Further, to deal with the Federation would complicate FTUI's work with the independents, who derive from it moral support as well as critical international recognition. And for what purpose would American aid be diluted by including the successor union grouping? As FTUI program officer Dan Rosenblum puts it, "They [the FNPR] don't need help."[57]

But the arguments for opening the educational component of FTUI's programs to interested FNPR unions, even if they have not formally broken away from the Federation, is more compelling. After several years of aid and development, the independents remain too small to represent more than a tiny fraction of the labor force. Only a few hundred thousand belong to unions that have been built from the ground up. Significant numbers of workers will be represented and defended properly during the transition period only if more of the existing unions democratize. More important, reformed FNPR unions can bring to the table organizational resources and expertise critical for effective collective bargaining and political influence that the independents cannot command. According to Pekko Aro, who has worked extensively on ILO programs in Russia, "The FNPR has the economic information and capability to analyze it that one finds in any trade union organization in the West."[58] The breakaway Mining and Metallurgical Workers' Union had an entire Division of Legal Protection to bring to "Rule of Law" seminars and work on legislative changes.

These thoughts are not intended to exaggerate the prospects for reform within the FNPR, only to make the case that the potential payoff of supporting any reformist elements is great. A number of circumstances are pushing these unions out of their entrenched position; seminars that introduce concepts of democratic unionism and leadership accountability could contribute to the "pull" away from old patterns of behavior. At least one scholar who has studied the FNPR-affiliated Coal Industry Workers' trade union concludes: "the mine level committees would benefit from trade union education. . . . [Union] officials have a strong survival instinct and they know that the union must reform. The best of the mine trade union committees want to learn."[59] Rosenblum is, of course, right that the FNPR does not need help in a material sense, but it does require exposure to democratic norms and collective bargaining procedures if it is going to reform.

A more open attitude toward FNPR unions would lessen perceptions that FTUI's efforts are partisan and deliberately divisive, and it possibly would facilitate coordination with other Western organizations that work with all unions. Indeed, Carothers concludes that aid givers should not write off even stagnant institutions but try to direct assistance to reform elements within them—it is better to offer ideas and knowledge to all willing recipients.[60] Some observers argue that the AFL-CIO's historical anti-Communism stands in the way of such a change in approach, but there is at least ambiguous evidence that FTUI is already moving in this direction for FNPR unions that display some militance, particularly at the local level.[61] The AFL-CIO's present policy clearly allows for such liberalization; according to Phillip Fishman, assistant director of the International Affairs Department, "For the AFL-CIO, the criterion for support is not a union's age, size, wealth or economic philosophy, but its democratic character; is it a *free* trade union, representing no other interest than that of its members."[62] Insofar as any FNPR unions seem willing to embrace this principle, they should be encouraged.

Some observers have questioned the appropriateness for Russia of the U.S. model of enterprise-level collective bargaining and an adversarial union-management relationship. They argue that a European model of government/business/labor cooperation and nationwide negotiating is more suited to Russia's centralist traditions and political culture.[63] But this tripartite model has worked poorly in Russia, with national-scale agreements vague, frequently ignored by the government, and generally irrelevant to the concerns of individual enterprises. In part this is because the Russian government is trying to extricate itself from the economy rather than to manage it, and there are at present no central employer organizations. In fact, plant-level bargaining may be better suited in particular to conditions in the newly developing private sector. It would be preferable not to prejudge the model of labor relations that is best for Russia or other transitional economies but to offer different choices and let those involved take what they find useful.

POLICY RECOMMENDATIONS

CONCENTRATE ON CONCRETE SKILLS, INFORMATION, AND SUSTAINABILITY

The United States now has several years of experience with an assistance effort that has had a modestly positive impact on the survival and development of Russia's independent trade unions. That effort has already been pared back greatly, with mainly its most effective components—the training and legal programs—surviving. These two programs provide the kinds of concrete skills and information that are most valued by Russian unionists and have the most tangible impacts. Even if more funds become available, the newly narrowed programmatic priorities should be retained; the media, research, and other projects attempted earlier are too amorphous, expensive, and of uncertain benefit. Future aid should concentrate on unions in their start-up phase, make it clear that these unions must progressively take over the functions performed by aid organizations, and avoid placing Russian union organizers on American payrolls. These measures should minimize the potential for union dependence on aid providers and discourage a sense of entitlement that can lead to disillusionment. FTUI seems the obvious organization to continue in the lead role because its personnel stay in Russia long enough to understand the situation there, it has developed a collaborative working relationship with local partners, and its programs are geared toward sustainability. Its present emphasis on "training trainers" who can continue union education programs without American aid is especially important, both because this approach enables local leaders and because the American commitment to future assistance remains tenuous.

COORDINATE WITH OTHER INTERNATIONAL ORGANIZATIONS

A number of Western organizations provide similar types of assistance to Russian trade unions, all on a modest scale. Each operates from a small office in Moscow, with outreach to unions in Russia's vast provinces. While these organizations occasionally cooperate in running a seminar or conference, they make little effort to communicate regularly or coordinate their activities. A great deal could be gained if they exchanged information, for example, about promising new union organizing initiatives, the potential for democratization within particular FNPR unions or regional organizations, or successful techniques in educational work. More important, joint arrangements could serve to maximize the impact of their limited resources, assuring that aid is distributed among as many receptive unions as possible rather than focused on a few that might seek it most aggressively. Coordination even among agencies of a single government is admittedly difficult; among international organizations with differing approaches it would surely be more so. But in its absence they are at risk of duplicating scarce efforts and repeating one another's mistakes.

EXPAND THE "RULE OF LAW" PROGRAM

The "rule of law" program provides one of the best prospects for Western assistance to build on indigenous developments in Russia, in this case, the passage of a body of legislation that protects labor's organizing and bargaining rights. When workers know their rights and have access to competent legal advice they often win in court. Regular enforcement of these rights, however, requires development of the legal profession—the introduction of new curricula into law schools and the training of a steady stream of labor and public interest lawyers. The United States already has programs in place, through AID and the American Bar Association, to support legal reforms and the creation of legal education programs.[64] One such program provides for the addition of commercial law courses to university offerings. Some of the available funding should be directed to designing labor law courses and developing curriculum. FTUI has already established contacts with Russian law schools through its legal offices, so it is in a good position to facilitate collaborative grant proposals with counterparts in the ABA. Other Western organizations, including the European Union's TACIS (Technical Assistance to the Commonwealth of Independent States), also have legal assistance programs that might contribute.[65] Assistance should be only for the start-up phase, with educational programs expected to become self-sustaining once they are in place.

The United States should consider providing more funds in the short term to the "rule of law" project, already in place, which helps inform workers about their new organizing and collective bargaining rights and enables independent unions to go to court over violations. The need is admittedly vast, but educational efforts can have a significant multiplier effect, spreading knowledge throughout the labor force. Even with awareness of their rights, however, most independents are too poor to contest many of the rampant violations they encounter. More access to legal services would help them to establish a record of legal judgments and a pattern of enforcement. If managers come to expect strict observance of legislated rights, they should be more likely to respect those rights and to bargain in good faith. Unions that can deliver, in court and in contract negotiations, would be better able to consolidate and attract new members.

ADD ECONOMIC AND TECHNICAL EXPERTISE

Any program of assistance to new Russian trade unions should include some provision of technical and economic expertise during contract negotiations.[66] Independent unions vitally need such expert advice to help them assess labor's prospects and bargain effectively with managements. Yet they often lack access to even basic intelligence about production costs, the prices their goods can command, the financial position of their enterprise, or international marketing opportunities.

Poor information has been very costly for Russia's independent unions, leading them to make unrealistic promises to their members and to raise expectations that are inevitably disappointed. Such false expectations undermine the credibility of union leaders and discourage workers from further organization and collective action.

Western aid organizations would contribute much to the viability of these unions by subsidizing expert consultations to prepare them for collective bargaining. Such help could be provided by the United States in cooperation with the ILO and TACIS, both of which already have other types of technical assistance programs. Consultants should come from the ranks of Russian economists, academics, and technical specialists. Unions need knowledge that is specific to their sectors and products in order to make realistic proposals and demands. They must be able to assess restructuring programs in privatized enterprises for technical feasibility and impact on labor, and to make informed objections and offer alternatives to managers' plans. Managers dominated the privatization process largely because of their control over information, and they will have a free hand in the reshaping of these enterprises unless unions have the resources and know-how to challenge them. Unions that lack the competence to bargain for their members are unlikely to survive.

IDENTIFY AND WORK TO EMPOWER PROREFORM ELEMENTS IN THE FNPR

Most knowledgeable observers believe that there are some reformist elements in the successor unions. FTUI should seek to identify these and, if they are receptive, include them in seminars and informational activities. The cost incurred to expose some FNPR workers to the concepts of democratic unionism and leadership accountability would be small, and the payoff could be great. The movement of some FNPR unions in a reformist direction could have a demonstration effect on others that are presently losing members and influence. If additional FNPR unions democratize, reject managerial dominance, and turn toward their rank and file, they would bring substantial legal, technical, and other resources to the defense of labor. If they do not, most of Russia's workers will have no effective trade unions during the transition period. Though the independents exert critical pressures for democratization, Western assistance efforts geared solely toward them are reaching far too few workers.

RELY ON AFL-CIO FUNDS

It would be preferable for the AFL-CIO to fund its own programs in Russia, in whole or in large part, rather than relying on government grants. Such a step would set aside any questions about FTUI's political independence in relation, for example, to the particulars of U.S.-supported economic stabilization programs. The evidence indicates that FTUI does act independently, but doubts will always remain if nothing changes, especially in the minds of some Russians who see the negative implications for labor of these stabilization prescriptions. Cost is of course an issue, but the newly resurgent AFL-CIO under John Sweeney is in a better position financially than in the recent past, even as government funding has declined precipitously. If a strong international labor movement to counter the globalization of capital is in the interest of American workers, the AFL-CIO should be willing to pay to promote it. It could begin by replacing the funds that FTUI has lost, and could seriously consider adding more.

EXPECT MODEST RESULTS FROM A MODEST INVESTMENT

Democratic trade unionism in Russia—either the development of independent unions or democratization of the FNPR—faces enormous obstacles, including the culture of workers' dependence, the weaknesses of legal norms, and the entrenched interests of many in the successor union federation. The United States and Western multilateral organizations are committing meager resources to the aid effort, from which should arise commensurately small gains: modest growth in or perhaps just the survival of independents, a little improvement in the responsiveness of FNPR officials to their members. Policymakers and the public should be led to expect no more.

CONCLUSION

Much else must be done before Russian trade unions will be able to defend their members adequately. The Russian government's regulatory capacities must be strengthened so that it can inspect facilities, enforce safety and other standards, and mediate conflicts between the major players in the economy. It must develop capabilities, both at the central and local levels, to take over administration of necessary social services and other functions long performed by enterprises. Both unions and government need advice on policies to deal with economic restructuring, development of labor markets, unemployment, poverty, and related issues. A number of Western organizations are already providing assistance in these areas, but a great deal more needs to be done. For much of it to be applicable requires that the Russian government first put its own house in order.

Ultimately, improvement in the position of most Russian workers will require the resumption of economic growth. But even resumed growth may bring few benefits to the majority if maldistribution, deep inequalities, and corruption continue to flourish. Effective trade unions can give large numbers of workers and citizens some say over the distribution of benefits, a collective voice in negotiating their future.

QUESTIONS FOR RUSSIAN INDEPENDENT TRADE UNIONISTS

1. First a few questions about [name of union]:

   A) How large is your union—what is its total membership?

   B) Where is it organized, i.e., in what regions or sectors?

   C) Has it grown over the past three years? How much?

2. How did your union first come in contact with the AFL-CIO's Free Trade Union Institute (FTUI)? Do you think that the main staff people there (i.e., former Director Tom Bradley, present Director Scott Reynolds, and others) understand the situation in Russia and the problems of your trade union well?

3. In which FTUI Programs have members of your trade union participated?

   A) attended seminars in labor organizing, union-building, collective bargaining, or more specialized topics?

   B) participated in RAFTURE meetings and programs

   C) consulted with lawyers or others at the Labor Law Centers ("Rule of Law" Project)

   D) received books and pamphlets on labor issues, the newspaper *Delo*, listened to radio programming

E) Trade Union Organizers and Interns work for your union

F) received communications equipment

G) any other programs or services

4.   If members of your union participated in any of these programs, please answer the following questions:

A) If members of your union participated in seminars:

- How many members from your union took part?

- Who chose the people to participate?

- Was the information taught in the seminars *useful* to your union, and if so, specifically, how:

  ◆ Did it help you to recruit new members or retain members?

  ◆ Did it help you in bargaining with management—in collective bargaining?

  ◆ Did it help you in building your union in other ways?

- Did people from your union help in planning seminars or deciding on their content?

- Are activists who receive training in such seminars able to teach their skills to others in the union?

- Do you think that more such seminars would be useful, or would you change them? What kinds of changes would you make?

B) for RAFTURE:

- Did anyone from your union sit on RAFTURE's Advisory Council?

- Did RAFTURE's activities help your union? If so, how? Did it provide useful contacts with other union leaders or with people outside the trade union movement?

C) If your union consulted with the Labor Law Offices:

- How often, and about what issues or problems? For example:

  ◆ problems with registration of the union at an enterprise?

- illegal dismissals of workers or forced leaves?

- collective bargaining or labor contract violations?

- other issues?

- Did lawyers from the Labor Law Centers ever bring a case to court for your union? If so, what was the issue, and was it resolved successfully?

- Do you think the Centers have helped independent unions lobby the government or influence Federal labor laws such as the Russian Federation Labor Code, Law on Collective Bargaining, etc.?

D) If you union received literature, *Delo*, etc.:

- Was the information useful? How, specifically?

E) Has your union used Organizers or Interns from FTUI?

- If so, have they been effective in bringing in new members?

- Have FTUI organizers interfered with your union's activities?

5. Have meetings, seminars, and information from FTUI helped your union make contact and cooperate with other independent unions? Does your union belong to a federation of unions? Did FTUI help in creating the federation?

6. In your view, has FTUI (now or in the past) supported Yeltsin's government and/or shock-therapy reform, or taken a generally pro-market position?

- If so, does your union agree with this position?

- Must the union agree with such a position in order to get support from FTUI, or is support given to independent unions without regard to politics?

7. Do you agree with FTUI's policy of no-contact with FNPR-affiliated unions? Should it help some FNPR unions?

- Does your union have to avoid contacts with FNPR unions in order to keep FTUI's support, even if it wants to cooperate with local FNPR unions?

8. Has FTUI asked the leadership of your union what types of programs or aid would be most useful?

    - Has it responded to any advice or criticism from your union?

    - Has it changed or adapted programs to your needs?

9. Have recent reductions in FTUI's programs affected your union? Have activists already learned enough organizing skills by now? Do you need more of the kinds of help FTUI has been providing? Which programs would you most like to see continued?

10. Has your union worked with other Western or international labor organizations (for example, European unions or the ILO)? If so, are their programs more or less useful than FTUI's? If more useful, why? Do the Americans and others work together? If not, would it be better if they did?

NOTES

INTRODUCTION

1. See *Izvestiya* (Moscow), December 30, 1993; Elizabeth Teague, "Who Voted for Zhirinovsky?" *RFE/RL Research Report* 3, no. 2, Radio Free Europe/Radio Liberty (January 14, 1994): 3.

2. "Report on the Russian Duma Elections of December, 1995," Commission on Security and Cooperation in Europe, Washington, D.C., March 1996, p. 17; "Competition between Regimes: Yeltsin vs. Zyuganov," in Stephen White, Richard Rose, and Ian McAllister, *How Russia Votes* (Chatham, N.J.: Chatham House Publishers, 1997), pp. 241–70. Nationalist issues, particularly resentment over Russia's loss of empire, also drive this vote.

3. U.S. Congress, House, Committee on International Relations, *Promoting Democracy: Progress Report on U.S. Democratic Development Assistance to Russia*, report to the chairman and ranking minority member, 104th Cong., 2d sess., February 1996, p. 33. When unions come to FTUI requesting assistance, staff review them to determine whether they meet the two criteria of being democratic and independent.

4. The description of FTUI's programs is based on two sources: cited interviews with those who administer the programs, both in Washington, D.C., and in Russia, and FTUI's quarterly reports to its funding agencies, AID, NED, and ARD/CHECCHI, for 1994–96.

5. Author telephone interview with Scott Reynolds, former executive director, Moscow Office, Free Trade Union Institute, June 27, 1996.

6. Author interview with Daniel Rosenblum, senior program officer for the former Soviet Union, Washington, D.C., December 19, 1995.

7. Further discussion of these interviews can be found in Chapter 5.

8. This point is made in Thomas Carothers, *Assessing Democracy Assistance: The Case of Romania* (Washington, D.C.: Carnegie Endowment for International Peace, 1996), p. 80.

9. See "Russian Presidential Election," in *Transitions* 2, no. 11 (May 31, 1996): 7–8, which recounts several incidents raising the specter that the elections might be delayed or canceled, including one in early May when Aleksandr Korzhakov, then chief of the Presidential Security Service, said he supported postponing the elections and predicted unrest whatever the outcome.

108   LABOR AND LIBERALIZATION

10. See *World Development Report 1995: Workers in an Integrating World* (New York: Oxford University Press, for the World Bank, 1995), pp. 81–82.

11. On this point, see Guy Standing, "Enterprise Restructuring in Russian Industry and Mass Unemployment: The RLFS Fourth Round, 1994," ILO Labour Market Papers no. 1, International Labor Organization, Geneva, p. 56.

CHAPTER ONE

1. Blair Ruble, *Soviet Trade Unions: Their Development in the 1970's* (New York: Cambridge University Press, 1981), pp. 2, 48; figures are for 1977.

2. Unions did make collective agreements with management at the enterprise level, but these largely applied centrally set wage and other policies and involved no real bargaining; see John Thirkell, Richard Scase, and Sarah Vickerstaff, eds., *Labor Relations and Political Change in Eastern Europe: A Comparative Perspective* (Ithaca, N.Y.: Cornell University Press, 1995), p. 9.

3. See Linda J. Cook, *The Soviet Social Contract and Why It Failed: Welfare Policy and Workers' Politics from Brezhnev to Yeltsin* (Cambridge, Mass.: Harvard University Press, 1993), pp. 73–76.

4. Bernice Q. Madison, "Trade Unions and Social Welfare," in Arcadius Kahan and Blair Ruble, *Industrial Labor in the USSR* (New York: Pergamon Press, 1979), pp. 85–116; Ruble, *Soviet Trade Unions*, pp. 49, 88.

5. Madison, "Trade Unions and Social Welfare," p. 93.

6. "Russia: Social Protection during Transition and Beyond," World Bank Report no. 11748-RU, World Bank, February 2, 1994, p. 139. The share of enterprise housing is highest in heavy and defense industries.

7. Cook, *Soviet Social Contract*, pp. 173–77.

8. John Lowenhardt, *The Reincarnation of Russia: Struggling with the Legacy of Communism* (Durham, N.C.: Duke University Press, 1995), p. 98. Both the disbanding of enterprise party cells and Yeltsin's ultimately temporary ban of the Communist Party and transfer of its property to the state after the August 1991 coup attempt caused much anxiety for the union, which feared that it might suffer a similar fate.

9. The major exceptions remain the coal and agricultural sectors.

10. See "Wage Formation during the Period of Economic Restructuring in the Russian Federation," Centre for Co-operation with the Economies in Transition OECD/GD(95) no. 102, Organization for Economic Cooperation and Development, Paris, 1995, pp. 17–20. Though wages recovered somewhat during 1992 and 1993 later drops neutralized these gains. The authors of this OECD study conclude that, by late 1994, real wages did not exceed 40 percent of their 1991 level.

11. See *Russian Economic Trends, Monthly Update*, April 22, 1996, p. 21. (*Russian Economic Trends* is produced by the Working Centre for Economic Reform, Government of the Russian Federation, with the assistance of the London School of Economics' Centre for Economic Performance team working within

the Russian European Centre for Economic Policy, and is published by Whurr Publishers, London.)

12. Working-age adults, with their families, form the bulk of the poor in Russia. Virtually all employees have income apart from wages. In fact, the share of wages in overall income has declined dramatically, from 82 percent in 1992 to a projected 41 percent in 1995. For data on the social composition of poverty in Russia, see "Wage Formation during the Period of Economic Restructuring," pp. 19, 38.

13. See ibid., p. 18; *Russian Economic Trends* 5, no. 2 (1996): 64.

14. See Guy Standing, "Enterprise Restructuring in Russian Industry and Mass Employment: The RLFS Fourth Round, 1994," ILO Labour Market Papers no. 1, International Labor Organization, Geneva, pp. 31–32. Standing's conclusions are based on data from large surveys rather than official statistics.

15. *OECD Economic Surveys: The Russian Federation, 1995* (Paris: Organization for Economic Cooperation and Development, 1995), pp. 143–54; Standing, "Enterprise Restructuring in Russian Industry," pp. 5–8.

16. See Peter Rutland, "Yeltsin Fires Top Social Welfare Officials," *OMRI Daily Digest*, no. 100, Open Media Research Institute, Prague, May 23, 1996, Part I.

17. Survey research shows that already in 1993, a majority of workers in state enterprises believed they faced the possibility of dismissal. An August 1995 survey by the All-Russian Center for the Study of Public Opinion (VTsIOM) showed that "rising unemployment" ranked third in the population's list of concerns, behind "rising prices" and "rising crime." See V. S. Magun and V. E. Gimpelson, "Strategii adaptatsii rabochikh na rynke truda" (Strategies of Workers' Adaptation to the Labor Market), *Sotsiologicheskiye Issledovaniya* (Moscow), no. 9 (1993): 73–83; *Russian Economic Trends* 4, no. 3 (1995): 92.

18. Foreign Broadcast Information Service Report: Soviet Union, Russian Affairs (hereafter, FBIS-USR) 91-061, December 27, 1991, pp. 29–30, citing *Trud.*

19. See Valentin Rupets, "Trade Union Movement in 'Post-Totalitarian Russia'" (classification essay), *New Labour Movement* (informational and analytical bulletin) nos. 3–4 (1992): 44.

20. For reports of these surveys, see *Delovoy Mir* (Moscow), May 10–16, 1994, pp. 14–15; *Rabochaya Tribuna* (Moscow), October 28, November 2, 6, 1993; *Current Digest of the Post-Soviet Press* 49, no. 3 (February 19, 1977): 2, citing *Nezavisimaya Gazeta.*

21. *Rossiyskaya Gazeta* (Moscow), February 7, 1992, p. 2.

22. Author interview with members of the Legal Commission of the Russian Federation of Free Trade Unions, Moscow, May 25, 1993.

23. See Foreign Broadcast Information Service Daily Report: Central Eurasia (hereafter, FBIS-SOV) 95–071, April 13, 1995, p. 35, citing ITAR-TASS. In April 1995, for example, the FNPR sponsored a nationwide day of protest. Reports on numbers participating varied; the minister of the interior cited 450,000, while FNPR claimed three times as many.

24. See, for example, *Trud* (Moscow), September 20, 1991, p. 1; *Rabochaya Tribuna* (Moscow), April 3, 1992, p. 3; *Rossiyskaya Gazeta* (Moscow), July 6, 1993, p. 5.

25. See, for example, *Rabochaya Tribuna* (Moscow), April 17, 1992, p. 1; *Trud* (Mosocw), March 21, 1992, p. 2; *Rabochaya Tribuna* (Moscow), April 5, 1994, p. 1.

26. *Rabochaya Tribuna* (Moscow), April 5, 1994, p. 1; FBIS-SOV-94-100, May 24, 1994, pp. 34–35, citing Interfax.

27. *Rossiyskiye Vesti* (Moscow), October 4, 1993, p. 1; *Argumenty i Fakty* (Moscow), November 14, 1994, p. 5.

28. See the presidential ukase "On Social Partnership and the Resolution of Labor Disputes" (November 15, 1991), published in *Trud* (Moscow), January 15, 1992.

29. Author interviews with Vladimir Makhanov, member of the Russian Federation Supreme Soviet Commission on Social Policy, Moscow, May 25, 1993, and Alexander K. Utkin, chairman of the Subcommission on the Population Level and Living Indexation, Russian Federation Supreme Soviet Commission on Social Policy, Moscow, May 26, 1993.

30. Walter Connor, *Tattered Banners: Labor, Conflict, and Corporatism in Post-communist Russia* (Boulder, Colo.: Westview Press, 1996), pp. 188–89. The bloc received slightly more than 1 million votes.

31. Simon Clarke, Peter Fairbrother, and Vadim Borisov, *The Workers' Movement in Russia* (Brookfield, Vt.: Edward Elgar Publishing Co., 1995), p. 407.

32. See T. Chetvernina, P. Smirnov, and N. Dunaeva, "Mesto Profsoiuza na predpriiatii" (The Place of Trade Unions at the Enterprise), *Voprosy Ekonomiki* (Moscow), no. 6 (June 1995): 83–84.

33. See *Kommersant-Daily* (Moscow), June 18, 1994, p. 3; *Segodnya* (Moscow), September 22, 1994, p. 3.

34. See, for example, FBIS-SOV-93-188-S, September 30, 1993, pp. 37–38, citing *Moskovskiy Komsomolets*; FBIS-SOV-93-212, November 4, 1993, p. 27, citing ITAR-TASS.

35. See the presidential decree "On Management of State Social Insurance in the Russian Federation" (September 28, 1993), reprinted in FBIS-SOV-93-187, September 29, 1993, p. 16, citing ITAR-TASS; on the dues collection ban by Vladimir Shumeiko, see Connor, *Tattered Banners*, p. 130.

36. In 1994 a multiyear study found that, while some enterprises had added new benefits, for the first time more had cut some benefits (28 percent) than added any; Standing, "Enterprise Restructuring in Russian Industry," p. 55. This trend continues. It should be noted, however, that in a high-inflation economy certain subsidies may be more valuable to workers than in the past even if overall levels of provision fall.

37. For the SIF's value, see *Russian Federation: Economic Review* (Washington, D.C.: International Monetary Fund, 1993), p. 18; *Russia: Social Protection during Transition and Beyond* (Washington, D.C.: World Bank, 1994), p. 33 (though one wonders whether the funds would be better managed under government control). In May 1996, Yeltsin fired Yuri Shatyrenko, head of the Social Insurance Fund, for mismanagement leading to abuse and financial instability of the fund.

38. See Cathy Cosman, "Labor Issues in Post-Soviet Society," unpublished paper given at the Kennan Institute for Advanced Studies, Washington, D.C., June 7, 1993, cited in Sue Davis, "State-Society Relations in Post-Soviet Systems: Trade Unions in Russia and Ukraine," paper presented at the annual conference of the American Association for the Advancement of Slavic Studies, Washington,

D.C., October 26–29, 1995, p. 6. There are no estimates of the extent of the FNPR's property, though it has been characterized as the richest social organization in Russia.

39. On the FNPR's dependence on government for retaining its power, privileges, and wealth, see Clarke, Fairbrother, and Borisov, *Workers' Movement in Russia*, pp. 406–7.

40. This is the term used by Stephen Crowley, in personal communication with the author, May 29, 1996.

41. Sarah Ashwin, "Russia's Official Trade Unions: Renewal or Redundancy?" *Industrial Relations Journal* 26, no. 3 (Summer 1995): 192–203; author telephone interviews with Pekko Aro, senior specialist for workers' activities, Central and Eastern Europe, International Labor Organization, Budapest, July 10, 1996, and Anna Oulatar, head of the Coordinating Unit for Central and Eastern Europe, International Confederation of Free Trade Unions, Brussels, June 1996.

42. There is, of course, no single Western model of trade unions. Some of the differences between American and European unions, and their significance for aid efforts in Russia, are discussed in Chapter 5.

43. The numbers reported vary. In February 1994, the chairman of the Social Insurance Fund claimed that some ninety trade unions were seeking representation on the Fund's management board; see *Rabochaya Tribuna* (Moscow), February 12, 1994, p. 2.

44. Author interview with Leonid A. Gordon, professor, Institute of World Economy and International Relations, and vice director for labor studies, Center for Socio-Political and Economic Studies, Moscow, May 28, 1993.

45. For many examples of such "wars of attrition," see Clarke, Fairbrother, and Borisov, *Workers' Movement in Russia*, especially chapter 5.

46. The point about higher education as a common feature of most occupations with strong independent unions was made by Leonid Gordon in an interview with the author, Moscow, May 28, 1993. According to Gordon, one-third of miners have some higher education, largely because exceptionally high wages for rank-and-file miners during the Soviet regime attracted lower-paid employees (engineers, etc.) from other professions.

47. *Rossiyskiye Vesti* (Moscow), August 20, 1993, p. 1.

48. For reports of investigations showing the frequent collapse of local Sotsprof branches, see Clarke, Fairbrother, and Borisov, *Workers' Movement in Russia*, pp. 246–54. Reports of strong regional organizations come from an author interview with Greg Schulze, director of organizing, Free Trade Union Institute, Moscow Office, Washington, D.C., June 20, 1996.

49. See *Moskovskiye Novosti* (Moscow), February 13–20, 1994, p. A11, where Sergeyev also cites the figure of 1 million miners in the FNPR.

50. Ashwin, "Russia's Official Trade Unions"; the quote is from p. 202.

51. Quote is from *Moskovskiye Novosti* (Moscow), February 13–20, 1994, p. A11.

52. See the interview with Misnik in *Novoye Vremya* (Moscow), no. 10 (March 1995): 18–19.

53. See *Segodnya* (Moscow), April 13, 1995, p. 2.

54. For example, the independents supported Yeltsin at the time of the April

1993 referendum on elections, calling on their members for a vote of confidence in the president and no confidence in the parliament that was thwarting his efforts; offered cooperation on putting together his constitutional commission; and backed his decision to dissolve the parliament in October 1993.

55. Stephen Crowley, "Barriers to Collective Action: Steelworkers and Mutual Dependence in the Former Soviet Union," *World Politics* 46, no. 4 (July 1994): 589–615. Crowley argues that miners were more militant because many fewer goods and services were provided to them through their places of work. See also Andrew G. Walder, *Communist Neo-Traditionalism: Work and Authority in Chinese Industry* (Berkeley, Calif.: University of California Press, 1986), especially chapters 1, 2.

56. Linda J. Cook and Vladimir E. Gimpelson, "Exit and Voice in Russian Managers' Privatization Strategies," *Communist Economies and Economic Transformation* 7, no. 4 (December 1995): 465–83.

57. Chetvernina, Smirnov, and Dunaeva, "Mesto Profsoiuza na predpriiatti," p. 83.

CHAPTER TWO

1. It has long been assumed that courts did play a strong role in enforcing labor rights during the Soviet period, though recent empirical research has cast doubt on this view. See Blair A. Ruble, *Soviet Trade Unions: Their Development in the 1970's* (New York: Cambridge University Press, 1981), pp. 64–89; Kathryn Hendley, *Trying to Make Law Matter: Legal Reform and Labor Law in the Soviet Union* (Ann Arbor, Mich.: University of Michigan Press, 1996).

2. See the law "On Amendments and Additions to the RSFSR Code of Labor Laws," no. 3542–I, September 25, 1992, reprinted in *Rossiyskaya Gazeta* (Moscow), October 6, 1992, pp. 4–6.

3. Klebanov was chairman of a trade union association, the Central Committee of Free Trade Unions; *Segodnya* (Moscow), January 14, 1994, p. 2.

4. The text of the decree is in *Rossiyskaya Gazeta* (Moscow), October 31, 1991, p. 2. It has been superseded by a new federal law, "On Public Associations," passed by the State Duma on April 14, 1995, and signed by Yeltsin on May 19; see FBIS Daily Report: Central Eurasia (hereafter, FBIS-SOV) 95-098, May 22, 1995, p. 29, citing ITAR-TASS.

5. "On Amendments and Additions to the RSFSR Code."

6. For the text, see "Rossiiskiya Federatsiya Federal'nii zakon: O profession-al'nykh soiuzakh, ikh pravakh, i garantiiakh deiatel'nosti'" (Russian Federation Federal Law: On Trade Unions, Their Rights, and Guarantees of Their Activities), December 18, 1995, published in *Rossiyskaya Gazeta* (Moscow), January 20, 1996, pp. 3–4.

7. *Annual Survey of Violations of Trade Union Rights 1994* (Brussels: International Confederation of Free Trade Unions, 1994), p. 85.

8. Author interview with members of the Legal Commission of the Russian Federation of Free Trade Unions, Moscow, May 25, 1993.

9. Simon Clarke, Peter Fairbrother, and Vadim Borisov, *The Workers' Movement in Russia* (Brookfield, Vt.: Edward Elgar Publishing Co., 1995), pp. 240–41.

10. "Third Quarterly Report to ARD/CHECCHI on the Rule of Law/Russia Project (February 1, 1995–April 30, 1995)" (xerox), Free Trade Union Institute, Washington, D.C., p. 7.

11. "Second Quarterly Report to ARD/CHECCHI on the Rule of Law/Russia Project (November 1, 1994–January 31, 1995)" (xerox), Free Trade Union Institute, Washington, D.C., pp. 2–3; Clarke, Fairbrother, and Borisov, *Workers' Movement in Russia*, pp. 222, 242.

12. See, for example, *Annual Survey of Violations of Trade Union Rights 1994*; Paul Gordon, "Russian Trade Unionism and the AFL-CIO," unpublished paper, School of Advanced International Studies, Johns Hopkins University, Spring 1994.

13. The text is in *Rossiyskaya Gazeta* (Moscow), April 28, 1992, p. 3; it also deals with collective agreements by profession, sector, or territory, though the procedures here are less clearly spelled out.

14. See *World Development Report 1995: Workers in an Integrating World* (Washington, D.C.: Oxford University Press for the World Bank, 1995), p. 82. The report states: "Legislation of limits on the number of unions per enterprise is viewed as an infringement on workers' rights. Union fragmentation and interunion rivalry are sometimes disruptive, however."

15. Author interview with Ellen Hamilton, program officer for the former Soviet Union, Free Trade Union Institute, Washington, D.C., June 19, 1996.

16. "The Social and Labour Situation in Russia 1993: Report of the Ministry of Labour of the Russian Federation," translated and annotated by David Mandel, *Labour Focus on Eastern Europe* (Oxford), no. 49 (Autumn 1994): 35–42.

17. See FBIS-SOV-94-189, September 29, 1994, p. 2, citing Interfax.

18. The commission was headed by Sergei Kovalyov; the relevant sections of the report are in *Nezavisimaya Gazeta* (Moscow), July 26, 1994, p. 6.

19. "Wage Formation during the Period of Economic Restructuring in the Russian Federation," Organization for Economic Cooperation and Development, Paris, 1995, p. 17.

20. Author interview with Thomas Bradley, executive director, Moscow Office, Free Trade Union Institute, Moscow, May 26, 1993.

21. "Wage Formation during the Period of Economic Restructuring," pp. 16–17.

22. See, for example, *Kommersant-Daily* (Moscow), March 12, 1994, p. 2.

23. In cases of collective labor disputes at these enterprises, trade unions could appeal to the president, prime minister, or highest official of the republic to make an executive decision on their demands.

24. The text is in *Izvestiya* (Moscow), May 30, 1991, p. 4; it was republished in the journal *Zakon* (Moscow), no. 6 (June 1993). The 1995 law is in *Rossiyskaya Gazeta* (Moscow), December 5, 1995, p. 4.

25. Two-thirds of the members of the organization must be present at the strike declaration.

26. See "Social and Labour Situation in Russia 1993," p. 40. Conciliation takes place between representatives of the parties to the dispute, while arbitration normally includes outsiders.

27. *Annual Survey of Violations of Trade Union Rights 1994*, p. 85.

28. Clarke, Fairbrother, and Borisov, *Workers' Movement in Russia*, pp. 339–57.

29. In the case of a 1994 pilots' strike, for example, the government went to court to have the strike declared illegal but negotiated anyway.

30. See "Wage Formation during the Period of Economic Restructuring," p. 17. One in ten would try to defend rights through strikes; the rest would seek further negotiations in the case of contract violations by management.

31. See Sergei Kovalyov's report in *Nezavisimaya Gazeta* (Moscow), July 26, 1994, p. 6.

32. See U.S. Congress, House, Committee on International Relations, *Promoting Democracy: Progress Report on U.S. Democratic Development Assistance to Russia*, report to the chairman and ranking minority member, 104th Cong., 2d sess., February 1996, p. 36.

33. On the miners' strikes, see Walter Connor, *The Accidental Proletariat: Workers, Politics, and Crisis in Gorbachev's Russia* (Princeton, N.J.: Princeton University Press, 1991); Theodore Friedgut and Louis Siegelbaum, "Perestroika from Below: The Soviet Miners' Strike and Its Aftermath," *New Left Review* 18, no. 1, 1990): 5–32; David Mandel, "The Rebirth of the Soviet Labour Movement: The Coalminers' Strike of July, 1989," *Politics and Society* 18, no. 3 (September, 1990): 381–404; Peter Rutland, "Labor Unrest and Movements in 1989 and 1990," *Soviet Economy* 6, no. 4 (October–December 1990): 345–84.

34. Quoted in FBIS-SOV-91-071, p. 44, April 12, 1991, citing Moscow All-Union Radio First Program, Radio-1 Network.

35. *Russian Economic Trends* 3, no. 2 (London: Whurr Publishers, 1994): 97.

36. *Pravda* (Moscow), January 25, 1992; *Izvestiya* (Moscow), May 16, 1992, p. 2; FBIS-SOV-95-186, September 26, 1995, pp. 66–67, citing ITAR-TASS.

37. At a protest by medical workers in sixty regions of Russia in the spring of 1996, for example, the deputy chair of the Union of Health Care Workers claimed that the 1996 federal budget allocation for health care covered only one-fifth of the sum requested by the Ministry of Health, and its inadequacy was causing shortages in medicine and equipment, the deterioration of treatment, and increases in infectious diseases and mortality rates; see Penny Morvant, "Health Workers Protest," *OMRI Daily Digest*, no. 73, Open Media Research Institute, Prague, April 12, 1996, Part I.

38. Personal observation by author, June 1992.

39. *Nezavisimaya Gazeta* (Moscow), January 6, 1994, p. 1; FBIS-SOV-94-003, January 5, 1994, pp. 37–38, citing *Krasnaya Zvezda*.

40. Quote is from FBIS-SOV-94-004, January 6, 1994, p. 39, citing Agence France Presse.

41. *Izvestiya* (Moscow), February 10, 1994, p. 1.

42. *Segodnya* (Moscow), May 25, 1994, p. 2; FBIS-SOV-94-196, October 11, 1994, p. 49, citing ITAR-TASS.

43. See, for example, Peter Rutland, "Workers Seize Weapons," *OMRI Daily Digest*, no. 100, Open Media Research Institute, Prague, May 23, 1996, Part I, for a report on a strike at a weapons plant to protest a five-month delay in wage payments.

44. See, for example, FBIS-SOV-95-025, February 7, 1995, p. 12, citing ITAR-TASS.

45. *Rossiyskaya Gazeta* (Moscow), February 3, 1994, p. 39.

46. *Izvestiya* (Moscow), November 4, 1994, p. 2.

47. Petr Biziukov, "The Social-Political Situation in the Kuzbass," *Labour Focus on Eastern Europe* (Oxford), no. 47 (Spring 1994): 36, introduced and translated by Simon Clarke.

48. FBIS-SOV-94-030, February 14, 1994, p. 39, citing Interfax.

49. See FBIS-SOV-96-022, February 1, 1996, p. 29, citing Moscow Radio Rossii Network. The miners also called for an end to the war in Chechnya, which they said was taking enormous resources from the program of civilian rebuilding in Russia.

50. See Ritsuko Sasaki, "Nationwide Miners Strike," *OMRI Daily Digest*, Open Media Research Institute, Prague, December 3, 1996, Part I; Penny Morvant, "Miners Suspend Strike," *OMRI Daily Digest*, Open Media Research Institute, Prague, December 12, 1996, Part I. The NPG opposed the strike, calling it "premature."

CHAPTER THREE

1. *Trud* (Moscow), February 25, 1992, pp. 1–2, translated in Foreign Broadcast Information Service: Central Eurasia, Russia, FBIS-USR-92-028, March 12, 1992, pp. 66–69.

2. The commission was established by a presidential ukase of November 15, 1991, "On Social Partnership and the Resolution of Labor Disputes (Conflicts)," *Vedomosti S'ezda narodnykh deputatov RSFSR I Verkhovnogo Soveta RSFSR*, no. 47, p. 1611, reprinted in *Zakon* (Moscow), no. 6 (June 1993): 58–59.

3. For the text, see *Ekonomika i Zhizn'* (Moscow), no. 17 (April 1992): 20.

4. *Trud* (Moscow), March 26, 1992, p. 1.

5. *Rabochaya Tribuna* (Moscow), March 24, 1992, p. 1.

6. The Civic Union took a moderately antireformist position, demanding that the government halt the decline in industrial production, guarantee employment, and maintain a large state role in the economy.

7. *Rabochaya Tribuna* (Moscow), December 18, 1992, p. 2; *Rossiyskiye Vesti* (Moscow), December 17, 1992, p. 5.

8. *Trud* (Moscow), February 25, 1992, pp. 1, 2.

9. Elizabeth Teague, "Russian Government Seeks 'Social Partnership,'" *RFE/RL Research Report* 1, no. 25, Radio Free Europe/Radio Liberty (June 19, 1992): 16–23.

10. *Trud* (Moscow), December 24, 1992, p. 1.

11. Elizabeth Teague, "Pluralism versus Corporatism: Government, Labor, and Business in the Russian Federation," in Carol R. Saivetz and Anthony Jones, *In Search of Pluralism: Soviet and Post-Soviet Politics* (Boulder, Colo.: Westview Press, 1994), p. 116.

12. The text of the agreement is in *Rabochaya Tribuna* (Moscow), May 7, 1993, pp. 3, 6.

13. Walter D. Connor, *Tattered Banners: Labor, Conflict, and Corporatism in Postcommunist Russia* (Boulder, Colo.: Westview Press, 1996), pp. 129–41.

14. The text is in *Izvestiya* (Moscow), April 30, 1994, p. 4.

15. Richard Freeman and James Medoff, *What Do Unions Do?* (New York: Basic Books, 1994), p. 38.

16. Author interview with a Social Democratic Party activist, Moscow, June 25, 1993.

17. See, for example, *Rossiyskaya Gazeta* (Moscow), September 10, 1993.

18. *Rossiyskaya Gazeta* (Moscow), December 8, 1993. The Agrarians won 47 of 450 seats in the Duma. Vera Tolz, "Russia's Parliamentary Elections: What Happened and Why," *RFE/RL Research Report* 3, no. 2, Radio Free Europe/Radio Liberty (January 14, 1994): 3.

19. *Izvestiya* (Moscow), October 27, 1993, p. 2; Tolz, "Russia's Parliamentary Elections," p. 3.

20. *Rossiyskiye Vesti* (Moscow), October 27, 1993, p. 2.

21. Vladimir E. Gimpelson, personal communication with the author, March 22, 1994.

22. See *Izvestiya* (Moscow), December 30, 1993, p. 4; Elizabeth Teague, "Who Voted for Zhirinovsky?" (sidebar) in Tolz, "Russia's Parliamentary Elections," pp. 4–5.

23. Petr Biziukov, "The Social-Political Situation in the Kuzbass," *Labour Focus on Eastern Europe* (Oxford), no. 47 (Spring 1994): 33, introduced and translated by Simon Clarke, cites a figure of 25.6 percent for Zhirinovsky's LDP versus 11.9 percent for Gaidar's Russia's Choice.

24. Timothy J. Colton, "The Russian Voter in 1993: Some Patterns in the National Survey Data," memorandum for the Russian Election Conference, Harvard University, April 9, 1994, pp. 12, 32.

25. See Connor, *Tattered Banners*, pp. 187–89; FBIS Daily Report: Central Eurasia (hereafter, FBIS-SOV) 95-214-S, November 6, 1995, pp. 29–32, citing *Segodnya*; FBIS-SOV-95-087, May 5, 1995, p. 16, citing *Segodnya*.

26. See FBIS-SOV-95-214-S, November 6, 1995, pp. 29–32, citing *Segodnya*; Connor, *Tattered Banners*, pp. 187–89.

27. Quote is from *Segondya* (Moscow), October 25, 1996, p. 3.

Chapter Four

1. Anders Åslund, *How Russia Became a Market Economy* (Washington, D.C.: Brookings Institution, 1995), pp. 223–71.

2. Quote is from *Ekonomicheskaya Gazeta* (Moscow), no. 19 (May 1992): 6; see also *Ekonomicheskaya Gazeta* (Moscow), no. 23 (June 1992): 14.

3. Linda J. Cook and Vladimir E. Gimpelson, "Exit and Voice in Russian Managers' Privatization Strategies," *Communist Economies and Economic Transformation* 7, no. 4 (December 1995): 465–83.

4. Roman Frydman et. al, *The Privatization Process in Russia, Ukraine, and the Baltic States* (New York: Central European University Privatization Project, 1993), pp. 51–58.

5. The energy and defense sectors, for example, were initially exempted from privatization, but enterprises from these sectors were included beginning in 1993.

6. See *Delovoy Mir* (Moscow), January 10–16, 1994, pp. 14–15.

7. Foreign Broadcast Information Service Report: Central Eurasia, FBIS-USR-93-069, June 4, 1993, pp. 34–38, citing *Trud.*

8. See *Izvestiya* (Moscow), February 23, 1993, p. 4; *Rossiyskiye Vesti* (Moscow), July 29, 1993, p. 2.

9. Åslund, *How Russia Became a Market Economy,* pp. 252–54; statistics are for the end of year 1993.

10. See A. Radygin, "Privatizatsiia i formirovanie novoi struktury sobstvennos-ti v Rossii: investitsionnyi aspekt" (Privatization and the Formation of New Ownership Structures in Russia: The Investment Aspect), *Voprosy Ekonomiki* (Moscow), no. 6 (1994): 40; Maxim Boyko, Andrei Shleifer, and Robert W. Vishny, "Privatizing Russia," paper prepared for Brookings Panel on Economic Activity, Brookings Institution, Washington, D.C., September 9–10, 1993, p. 34. There are no systematic national data available on management and other shareholder ownership.

11. See Joseph Blasi, Maya Kroumova, and Douglas Kruse, *Kremlin Capitalism: Privatizing the Russian Economy* (Ithaca, N.Y.: Cornell University Press, 1997), pp. 58–67, 193; *Russian Economic Trends* 5, no. 2 (London: Whurr Publishers, 1996): 117. Again, no systematic data were available.

12. *Russian Economic Trends* 5, no. 2 (London: Whurr Publishers, 1996).

13. Blasi, Kroumova, and Kruse, *Kremlin Capitalism,* p. 56, found that the number of companies in which managers owned large, concentrated shares of 20 to 40 percent increased substantially from 1995 to 1996 and that instances in which managerial ownership exceeded 48 percent of shares comprised more than 5 percent of all Russian companies and that for one in ten companies the level of the managers' stake approached or topped 40 percent.

14. See Simon Clarke et al., "The Privatization of Industrial Enterprises in Russia: Four Case Studies," *Europe-Asia Studies* 46, no. 2 (1994): 179–214 (n.b.: these are not typical enterprises; all were privatized early); Katharina Pistor, "Privatization and Corporate Governance in Russia: An Empirical Study," in Michael McFaul and Tova Perlmutter, eds., *Privatization, Conversion, and Enterprise Reform in Russia* (Stanford, Calif.: Center for International Security and Arms Control, May 1994), p. 76.

15. Pistor, "Privatization and Corporate Governance in Russia," p. 76.

16. Blasi, Kroumova, and Kruse, *Kremlin Capitalism,* p. 107.

17. Clarke et al., "Privatization of Industrial Enterprises in Russia."

18. See the case of the Saratov Airplane Factory in John Battilega, "A Case Study of Russian Defense Conversion and Employee Ownership," in McFaul and Perlmutter, *Privatization, Conversion, and Enterprise Reform in Russia,* pp. 169–88.

19. Clarke et al., "Privatization of Industrial Enterprises in Russia."

20. See *Ekonomika i Zhizn'* (Moscow), no. 5 (February 1996): 34.

21. Clarke et al., "Privatization of Industrial Enterprises in Russia"; David Mandel, "The Russian Working Class, Privatisation, and Labour-Management Relations in the Fourth Year of Shock Therapy," *Labour Focus on Eastern Europe* (Oxford), no. 52 (Summer 1995): 23–55.

22. Clarke et al., "Privatization of Industrial Enterprises in Russia."

23. In the Soviet Union, prior to this point few private economic activities were legal, though there was an extensive illegal private economy or black market.

24. Åslund, *How Russia Became a Market Economy*, pp. 263–64; Goskomstat Rossii (Russian State Statistical Committee), *Sotsial'no-ekonomicheskoe polozhenie Rossii* (The Socio-Economic Position of Russia), no. 12 (December 1995): 129–31.

25. See, for example, Mandel, "Russian Working Class, Privatisation, and Labour-Management Relations."

26. "Special Report: Labour Market Adjustment in Russia," *Russian Economic Trends* 3, no. 2 (London: Whurr Publishers, 1994): 85–95.

27. John R. Guardiano, "The Quest for a Social Safety Net: How Unemployed Are Russia's Unemployed?" *Russia's Social Problems: A Report by the Center for American-Eurasian Studies and Relations* (Washington, D.C.), a freestanding report in the series *Eurasian Reports* 4, no. 1 (Winter 1994–95): 73–75.

CHAPTER FIVE

1. The description of FTUI's programs is based mainly on two sources: cited interviews with those who administer the programs, both in Washington, D.C., and in Russia; and the FTUI's Quarterly Reports to its funding agencies, AID, NED, and ARD/CHECCHI for 1994–96.

2. Author interview with Ellen Hamilton, program officer for the former Soviet Union, Free Trade Union Institute, Washington, D.C., December 18, 1995.

3. Author interview with Thomas Bradley, former executive director, Free Trade Union Institute Moscow Office, Moscow, May 26, 1993. Of those interviewed, including a number of academic labor specialists, Bradley was probably the best informed about the overall status of the independents.

4. See, for example, "Performance Report to the U.S. Agency for International Development" (for the period August through December 1994), xerox, Free Trade Union Institute, Washington, D.C., no date, especially pp. 12–19.

5. Author interview with Daniel Rosenblum, senior program officer for the former Soviet Union, Free Trade Union Institute, Washington, D.C., December 19, 1995.

6. Interview with Hamilton. The offices were established in 1994 with a $195,000 grant from the NED's Worker Rights Project; see U.S. Congress, House, Committee on International Relations, *Promoting Democracy: Progress Report on U.S. Democratic Development Assistance to Russia*, report to the chairman and ranking minority member, 104th Cong., 2d sess., February 1996, p. 36. The $500,000 is from AID.

7. Author telephone interview with Scott Reynolds, former executive director, Free Trade Union Institute, Moscow Office, June 27, 1996; "1st Quarterly Report to ARD/CHECCHI, Rule of Law/Russia Project (August 17–October 31, 1994)," xerox, Free Trade Union Institute, Washington, D.C., no date; Fourth

Quarterly Report to ARD/CHECCHI, Rule of Law/Russia Project" (May 1–July 31, 1995)," xerox, Free Trade Union Institute, Washington, D.C., no date.

8. As of February 1996; see U.S. Congress, *Promoting Democracy*, p. 36.

9. "Second Quarterly Report to ARD/CHECCHI, Rule of Law/Russia Project (November 1, 1994–January 31, 1995)," xerox, Free Trade Union Institute, Washington, D.C., no date, pp. 1–2.

10. Interview with Hamilton.

11. "Fourth Quarterly Report to ARD/CHECCHI, Rule of Law/Russia Project (May 1–July 31, 1995)," xerox, Free Trade Union Institute, Washington, D.C., no date, pp. 1, 4.

12. "Performance Report for July–December, 1995: Russian-American Foundation for Trade Union Research and Education," xerox, Free Trade Union Institute, Washington, D.C., no date.

13. Interview with Reynolds.

14. Interview with Hamilton.

15. Interview with Reynolds; "Russsian Democratic Workers' Organizations, April 1, 1994-March 31, 1995," xerox, Free Trade Union Institute report to the National Endowment for Democracy, Washington, D.C., submitted March 17, 1995 (revised).

16. See, for example, Renfrey Clarke, "The American AFL–CIO in the Russian Labour Movement," *Labour Focus on Eastern Europe* (Oxford), no. 48 (Summer 1994): 84–92.

17. Dan Rosenblum explains that the organizers' component of the program was inspired by an approach used successfully by the CIO in the United States during the 1930s to break into new regions and industries.

18. U.S. Congress, *Promoting Democracy*, pp. 32–36.

19. However, Kudiukin stayed in the position only briefly, for reasons that are unclear. He remains active in a rather obscure political party of social-democratic orientation.

20. "Russian Democratic Trade Union Newspaper *Delo:* 'Prolog Society' (*Delo* newspaper)," April 1, 1995–March 31, 1996, Free Trade Union Institute, Washington, D.C., submitted January 15, 1995.

21. "Quarterly Report to the National Endowment for Democracy" (for the period January 1–March 31, 1995), xerox, Free Trade Union Institute, Washington, D.C., no date. The activities of the American Federation of Teachers are discussed within this report, pp. 86–96.

22. "Russian Democratic Workers' Organizations," item no. 6.

23. "International Labour Organization: Assistance to Central and Eastern Europe (including Central Asia) in 1995 to 1997," xerox, International Labor Organization, Geneva, no date, pp. 15–16; *Activities of the ILO, 1994–95: Report of the Director-General* (International Labor Conference, 83d session), International Labor Organization, Geneva, 1996, pp. 32–35, 162–67.

24. Author telephone interview with Pekko Aro, senior specialist for workers' activities, Central and Eastern Europe, Budapest Office, International Labor Organization, July 10, 1996.

25. *Programme and Budget for the Biennium, 1996–97* (Geneva: International Labor Organization, 1995), pp. 280–83.

26. Author telephone interview with Anna Oulatar, head of the coordinating unit for Central and Eastern Europe, International Confederation of Free Trade Unions, Brussels, June 1996.

27. Author telephone interview with Alexander Kallweit, head of projects on Russia, Ukraine, and the Baltics, Friedrich Ebert Institute, Bonn, July 18, 1996.

28. These interviews were conducted during the spring of 1996 in various parts of Russia by Victor Komarovsky of the Institute of World Economy and International Relations, Moscow. A copy of the interview questions is provided in Appendix A. The following leaders of independent trade unions were interviewed:

1) V. Vasil'ev, chairman of the Russian Trade Union of Dockers, April 25

2) A. Shepel, vice-chairman of the Russian Trade Union of Dockers, April 25

3) M. Tarasenko, chairman of the Union of Mining and Metallurgical Workers, April 30

4) E. Lichman, head of the international department, Union of Mining and Metallurgical Workers, April 30

5) A. Sergeev, chairman of the Independent Miners' Union of Russia (NPG); president of the All-Russian Confederation of Labor (VKT), April 22

6) E. Kinstler, former secretary-treasurer of the NPG, June 12

7) A. Kochurov, president of the Association of Flight Personnel, Federation of Free Trade Unions of Flight Personnel of Russia, April 29

8) S. Khramov, chairman of the Sotsprof Association of Trade Unions of Russia, April 23

9) V. Pivnov, vice president of the Federation of Air Traffic Controllers' Unions (FPAD), May 7

10) I. Koval'chuk, assistant to the president of the Russian Seafarers' Trade Union, June 5

11) G. Borisov, main vice president of the Association of Flight Personnel, Federation of Free Trade Unions of Flight Personnel of Russia; vice president of the Confederation of Free Trade Unions in Transport of Russia; vice president of the Confederation of Labor of Russia (KTP), April 29

12) L. Lerman, vice chairman of the Nizhegorodsky Regional Union of Sotsprof, April 23.

29. This point is made by Thomas Carothers in *Assessing Democracy Assistance: The Case of Romania* (Washington, D.C.: Carnegie Endowment for International Peace, 1996).

30. Interview with Shepel.

31. Interview with Lerman.

32. Interview with Kochurov.

33. Interview with Khramov.

34. Interview with Pivnov.

35. See, for example, the interview with Sergeev.

36. The Mining and Metallurgical Workers' Union is actually the largest, but it is a breakaway from the FNPR while both Sotsprof and the NPG were built from the grass roots.

37. Interview with Sergeev.
38. Interview with Khramov. For example, at the end of his interview Khramov said, apparently speaking of a grant proposal: "If FTUI had lobbied for and won our side with the Ford Foundation, then all of the financial problems of our unions would have been already solved. Then we would not have needed any other assistance from FTUI."
39. Various interviews with the trade union leaders.
40. See, for example, Lee H. Hamilton (D.-Ind.), ranking minority member of the House Committee on International Relations, "The Debate on Aid to Russia," *Problems of Post-Communism* 42, no. 3 (May–June 1995): 36–40.
41. U.S. Congress, House, *American Overseas Interest Act of 1995: Report of the Committee on International Relations*, H.R. 1561, 104th Cong., 1st sess., May 19, 1995, pp. 77–79.
42. Carothers, *Assessing Democracy Assistance*; Janine R. Wedel, "U.S. Aid to Central and Eastern Europe: Results and Recommendations," *Problems of Post-Communism* 42, no. 3 (May–June 1995): 45–50; Carothers points to a common failure "to develop activities as truly collaborative ventures in which local partners play an active role in planning and implementing assistance." See also Nancy E. Popson, "Foundation Assistance to Higher Education in Central Europe: What Has Worked Where and Why?" paper presented at the 28th annual convention of the American Association for the Advancement of Slavic Studies, Boston, November 14–17, 1996.
43. Author telephone interview with Nadia Diuk, regional director for Central and Eastern Europe and the Newly Independent States, National Endowment for Democracy, Washington, D.C, January 22, 1996; interview with Hamilton.
44. U.S. Congress, *Promoting Democracy*, p. 32.
45. Interviewed trade union leaders commented favorably on the Russian language competence of FTUI's new country director, Irina Stevenson.
46. Various interviews with the trade union leaders.
47. Carothers, *Assessing Democracy Assistance*, lists the "basic rules of development assistance" as local presence, local ownership of projects, local capacity building, and sustainability.
48. For a critical view of AIFLD from a leftist perspective, see Hobart A. Spalding, Jr., "US Labour Intervention in Latin America: The Case of the American Institute for Free Labor Development," in Roger Southall, ed., *Trade Unions and the New Industrialization of the Third World* (Pittsburgh: University of Pittsburgh Press, 1988), pp. 259–86. For a more balanced view, see Paul G. Buchanan, "The Impact of U.S. Labor," in Abraham F. Lowenthal, ed., *Exporting Democracy: The United States and Latin America* (Baltimore: Johns Hopkins University Press, 1991), pp. 296–330.
49. Buchanan, "Impact of U.S. Labor," p. 324. According to Buchanan, increased international competition "prompted U.S. labor to accept political, classist, and militant unions in Latin America, because it believes that the latter will deter or constrain U.S. investors, equalize labor climates worldwide, promote 'fair' trading practices, and thereby protect rank-and-file material interests at home."

50. Author telephone interview with Caroline Lauer, director of international affairs, Service Employees' International Union, AFL-CIO, Washington, D.C., July 17, 1996. According to Lauer, criticism within the AFL-CIO over its international policies "lapsed with the end of the cold war."

51. Clarke, "American AFL-CIO in the Russian Labour Movement," p. 92

52. Interview with Kochurov.

53. Interview with Pivnov.

54. Author interview with Boris Misnik, former president, Trade Union of Mining and Metallurgical Workers of Russia, Moscow, June 1, 1993; the present head of the metallurgical union, however, does favor a more cooperative relationship between FTUI and the FNPR.

55. Interview with Pivnov.

56. Carothers, *Assessing Democracy Assistance*, p. 92.

57. Interview with Rosenblum.

58. Interview with Aro.

59. Sarah Ashwin, "Russia's Official Trade Unions: Renewal or Redundancy?" *Industrial Relations Journal* 26, no. 3 (Summer 1995): 203.

60. Carothers, *Assessing Democracy Assistance*.

61. Scott Reynolds indicated a liberalization in attitude, and Anna Oulatar of the ICFTU said that FTUI had become more open to the idea of working with the FNPR, but FTUI's director of organizing for Russia stressed the FNPR unions' continuing subordination to management and dismissed the possibility of working with them; author interviews with Reynolds, Oulatar, and Greg Schulze, director of organizing, Moscow Office, Free Trade Union Institute, Washington, D.C., June 20, 1996.

62. Phillip Fishman, "Trade Unions in the Former Soviet Bloc," *Forum: The AFL-CIO Journal of International Affairs* 9, no. 2 (Winter/Spring 1995): 13.

63. See, for example, Carothers, *Assessing Democracy Assistance*, p. 80.

64. U.S. Congress, *Promoting Democracy*, pp. 47–49.

65. *Guide to TACIS Framework Programs: What They Are and How to Apply* (Brussels: Technical Assistance to the Commonwealth of Independent States, European Commission, December 1995), pp. 10–11.

66. This proposal comes originally from Ellen Hamilton of FTUI.

INDEX

ABOUT THE AUTHOR

L inda J. Cook is associate professor of political science at Brown University and a faculty associate of the university's Watson Institute for International Studies. She is also a fellow of the Davis Center for Russian Studies at Harvard University. She previously authored *The Soviet Social Contract and Why It Failed: Welfare Policy and Workers' Politics from Brezhnev to Yeltsin* (Harvard University Press, 1993), as well as articles in *Soviet Studies, Communist and Post-Communist Studies, Communist Economies and Economic Transformation,* and other journals and books. Ms. Cook has traveled several times to the former Soviet Union and the Russian Federation to conduct research and interviews. She is a member of the Social Science Research Council's Title VIII Program Committee and has served on an advisory panel at the Academy for Educational Development, which advises on a government-sponsored exchange program between U.S. and Russian universities. She received her Ph.D. from Columbia University and taught previously at Smith College.